LAST-MINUTE LITURGIES

Creating Prayerful Responses to the Unexpected

Donna M. Cole

Resource Publications, Inc.
San Jose, California

Reprint Department
Resource Publications, Inc.
160 E. Virginia St. #290
San Jose, California 95112-5876
(408) 286-8505
(408) 287-8748 fax

Library of Congress Cataloging-in-Publication Data

Cole, Donna, 1962-
  Last-minute liturgies : creating prayerful responses to the unexpected / by Donna M. Cole.
    p. cm.
  Includes bibliographical references.
  ISBN 0-89390-588-7
    1. Catholic Church--Liturgy. 2. Occasional services--Catholic Church. I. Title.

BX1970.C653 2003
264'.02--dc21

                                                          2003046622

Printed in the United States of America
03 04 05 06 07 | 5 4 3 2 1

Production staff: Nelson Estarija, Elizabeth Gebelein, Susan Carter

Dedicated to the members of the real Liturgical Emergency Response Team (whose mission continues today) with gratitude for their constant joy in liturgy, commitment to the ministry of the assembly, faith in the presence of the living God, and endless sense of humor. May our journey continue.

CONTENTS

ACKNOWLEDGMENTS. VII

PREFACE. 1

INTRODUCTION. 5

ABBREVIATIONS. 9

CHAPTER 1
UNDERSTANDING LITURGY 11
CHAPTER 2
WHERE TO BEGIN. 17
CHAPTER 3
RESOURCES AND HOW TO USE THEM
AT THE LAST MINUTE. 27
CHAPTER 4
ENVIRONMENT: STUFF TO USE TO CREATE
A PRAYERFUL SPACE AND HOW TO ARRANGE IT 55
CHAPTER 5
HOW TO LOOK LIKE YOU KNOW
EXACTLY WHAT YOU'RE DOING 65

CONCLUSION 83

BIBLIOGRAPHY. 85

RESOURCES. 87

Acknowledgments

Excerpts form the *Lectionary for Mass for Use in the Dioceses of the United States of America, second typical edition* © 1998, 1997, 1970, Confraternity of Christian Doctrine, Inc., Washington, DC. Used with permission. All rights reserved. No portion of this text may be reproduced by any means without permission in writing from the copyright owner.

Excerpts from *The Study of Liturgy, Second Edition,* edited by Cheslyn Jones, et al., © 1978 by Cheslyn Jones Geoffrey Wainwright and Edward Yarnold SJ, 1992 by Geoffrey Wainwright, Edward Yarnold SJ, and Paul Bradshaw. Used by permission of Oxford University Press, Inc.

Excerpts from the English translation of *The Roman Missal* © 1973, International Committee on English in the Liturgy, Inc.; excerpts from the English translation of *Eucharistic Prayers for Masses of Reconciliation* © 1975, ICEL; excerpts from the English translation of *Book of Blessings* © 1988, ICEL. All rights reserved.

Excerpts reprinted from "Theology of the Liturgy" by Alceste Catella, and "Liturgy and Spirituality" by Jesus Castellano Cervera, OCD. *Handbook for Liturgical Studies: Fundamental Liturgy* edited by Anscar J. Chupungco, © 1998 The Liturgical Press; excerpts reprinted from *Contemplative Participation: Sacrosanctum Concilium—Twenty-five Years Later* by Mary Collins, © 1990, TLP; excerpts reprinted from *On Liturgical Theology* by Aidan Kavanagh, © 1984, TLP. Used by permission.

Preface

Responding in prayer to an urgent situation is nearly a reflex. Even people who claim no connection to any faith tradition are likely to exclaim "Oh my God!" when confronted with crisis or tragedy. This may or may not be actual prayer, but nevertheless it has the effect of invoking the name of God, which is a large part of any act of prayer. In fact, in situations of crisis and tragedy many of the people who are most drawn to common prayer are those who have wandered from formal faith traditions. Part of the reason this book evolved was to support the efforts of so many people who stepped into leadership roles in the hours, days, and months immediately following the terrorist attacks of September 11, 2001. The desire for prayer at that time stood beside an unprecedented sense of national unity. Unusual prayer needs arose and unusual leaders stepped up to tend to those needs. Here in the New York metropolitan area, people joined in prayer while standing in the endless lines waiting to give blood for the wounded who never materialized. They prayed on street corners lit by candlelight and draped in flags and they sang songs that spoke of unity, pride, and hope. My own experience during that time was, and continues to be, transformative. Within hours following the first attack on the World Trade Center in New York City, I left the safety of my "ordinary" world, along with so many others, to respond to the tragedy that was unfolding. I serve with the United States Coast Guard Auxiliary, the volunteer component of the Coast Guard, and I soon found myself in New York Harbor in the midst of every human emotion. Pain, fear, confusion and dread were tangible but the worst of all of that was the simple unknown. We didn't know what to expect, what would come next, what we should try to defend against, how many might survive. Most of all we didn't know what to do or what to say. I have what once seemed to many to be an odd custom. Along with my life vest, my safety and survival gear, my charts, compass, radio, extra uniforms and all the other usual equipment we all carry, I carry the *Liturgy of the Hours* in my gear bag. On that day and on the days that followed, when there were no words, that book, the universal prayer of the church, gave me the words that I needed and that others needed to hear. Several months earlier, I had been appointed chaplain for my unit; in that time and place I became a chaplain. Thomas Merton, throughout his many journals, speaks of the challenge of learning to be the person you have become. This experience was a prime example of that evolution. Years of speaking the language of faith helped, my own faith experience helped, having a book of prayer in my hands helped; yet still, when faced with the explosions and pillars of smoke and the knowledge of wasted human life, my own first response was still, "Oh my God." And then my God answered me. What came next was both the ability and the desire to lead others in finding ways to interact with God in the unexpected moments of life. I am a pastoral minister by vocation, a chaplain by circumstance, and a lover of liturgy. Because of this, I was called upon to lead prayer as all of us in uniform prayed for strength, courage, and the safety of ourselves and our nation. At home I was inundated with requests from people in all stages of the faith journey for prayer services and vigils, memorials, and prayers of consolation. People wanted to pray spontaneously but they also wanted material that would speak to the needs of all who gathered to pray.

They were looking for symbols that had stood the test of time as well as those that would have to be created just for that moment and place. They were looking for the words, the poetry, the music that would reflect the intensity of the emotion of the time. In short, they were looking for the resources that this book offers. Given the currently changing face of ministry, especially liturgical ministry, many of those people seeking answers were (and continue to be) persons whose formal training in liturgy was limited but who were nevertheless leaders of prayer. Many of these were laypeople. Fearful of doing "the wrong thing," yet recognizing the urgency of the need, they rose to the occasion.

Thankfully, most of the unexpected events to which we are called to respond in prayer are events with far less global impact. Although our prayer responses may reflect sadness we are also called at times to reflect the joy and playfulness that our God delights in sharing with us. Although the inspiration for this book was a profoundly tragic event, most of my experiences of responding to the unexpected have been joyful. Even if the event was one that provoked sadness, the process of preparing for and engaging in prayer always happens in the place that God has prepared for me. In that place, God and I rejoice.

INTRODUCTION

THE LITURGICAL EMERGENCY

Beeeeeeeeeeeeep! "This is a test of the emergency liturgical broadcast system. In the event of an actual liturgical emergency, a Liturgical Emergency Response Team (LERT) would be dispatched to resolve the crisis. Resources would be gathered, music would be selected, liturgical texts would be chosen, ministers would be assigned, and worship aids would be produced. Prayer would be formed to match the context of the liturgical emergency, meeting the needs of the prayer community with sensitivity and grace. This broadcast has been brought to you by pastoral musicians, liturgy coordinators, presiders, other liturgical ministers, and all who work to enable prayerful experiences for all. Thank you for your attention."

If you have ever been confronted with a genuine liturgical emergency (and who hasn't?) you might have wished that LERT could have responded to your need. Actually, such a group does exist, but with a little proactive work, it is possible for anyone with some liturgical training to achieve the same prayer-filled result. Suddenly realizing that you are responsible for an unexpected liturgy can be challenging, but in actuality, being prepared for liturgical emergencies is easier than it seems. You'll find in this book the tools, the very nuts and bolts, you need to put together last-minute liturgies that work. Here's how to begin. First, don't panic. Not giving in to panic is the first step. Having the tools on hand to deal with last-minute liturgies is a little like having a first aid kit. With the right equipment you can improvise a solution to almost any situation.

Second, after you've calmed down from the initial shock, consider the goal. Starting with the goal in mind is crucial. The general goal of all liturgy is to enter more deeply into a relationship with God, but the particular goal of any given liturgy is generally more specific. For example, if you're preparing some sort of memorial service, the goal might be to provide an environment where grief and mourning can be supported by communal prayer. In this case, you would want to use texts, imagery, and environmental elements that speak of hope and peace while respecting the pain and sadness that is present. Using familiar music chosen from a common repertoire can provide an element of comfort that can help in the healing process.

Third, use what works and don't be afraid to steal! If you know of a service, song, or other liturgical element that has worked well for others, use it. Of course, if you do this, respect the work of others by giving credit wherever it is indicated and obey all copyright laws. But there is no need to reinvent the wheel if you know of something that works well. For example, if someone asks you to prepare a blessing for a parish group leaving for a trip somewhere, grab the *Book of Blessings* and use it! Adaptation is good and necessary, but if the poetry exists, use it.

Fourth, whenever possible, use a team approach to preparing liturgy. Don't try to do everything yourself. So if you happen to be a good presider, and you play an instrument, and your voice projects well, don't think that it's a good idea to preside, play, and preach at the same liturgy! Be the harmony, not the lead instrument. Liturgy is about participation, and the more participation you can encourage at every level, the more profound the result will be.

Last — always, always use sound liturgical principles in your preparation. This does not mean that you should be rigidly rubrical in your approach, but liturgy is a delicate entity that should always be treated with respect. The liturgical experience should always be such that it is worthy of the "Amen" of the assembly.

Having said all of that, it really is important to first ask the question, "What exactly is liturgy?" The "answer" given in this book is by no means complete, but it is at least sufficient to form the foundation for the topics discussed in each section. **(If you need quick answers, skip to chapter 2: "Where to begin.")**

Abbreviations

SC
Sacrosanctum Concilium

BB
Book of Blessings

CHBP
Catholic Household
Blessings & Prayers

NAB
New American Bible

CHAPTER 1

Understanding Liturgy

Using only words to describe liturgy is as difficult as attempting to describe the beauty and power of a blizzard to someone who has never seen a snowflake. A blizzard can be photographed, the sound of the winds can be recorded, the temperatures can be noted, the depth of the snow can be measured, and the casualties can be listed. These descriptive entities can be combined to construct an image of a blizzard, but that image is hollow, for the image lacks the essential substance of experience. To experience the biting cold winds, to feel the icy sting of the driven snow, to trudge through the snowdrifts, to "hear" the silence that comes from a blanket of deep snow, and to witness the blinding pure whiteness after the storm is to know, and therefore be able to define, a blizzard. Words fail, and so it is with liturgy. Liturgy can be partially defined in many different ways, but only through an experience of liturgy is the definition complete. Liturgy does not exist without experience; it is born and animated in the lived experience of the assembly of believers.

That experience has many dimensions, and the dynamic nature of liturgy makes a definition composed of inflexible words particularly challenging. "The liturgy is not something static, or a mental memorial, a model, a principle of action, a form of self-expression, or an escape into angelism. It reaches far beyond the signs in which it manifests itself and its effectiveness. It is not reducible to its celebrations, although it is indivisibly contained in them" (Corbon 67). In those celebrations, it is the presence and participation of the assembly that bring liturgy to life. "What results from a liturgical act is not only 'meaning,' but an ecclesial transaction with reality, a transaction whose ramifications escape over the horizon of the present, beyond the act itself, to overflow even the confines of the local assembly into universality. The act both changes and outstrips the assembly in which it occurs. The assembly adjusts to that change, becoming different from what it was before the act happened" (Kavanagh 78).

The experience of liturgy reaches beyond the limits of the actual celebration and has a transformative effect on the assembly, which in turns brings the assembly, and its subsequent worship, to a new level of experience. This is the beginning of a definition, that liturgy is a dynamic entity whose nature includes an essential transformative element. In addition, liturgy could be defined by this summary, "SC states that Christ is present in liturgical actions (no. 7); that the liturgy is a realization of the mystery of Christ by the power of the Holy Spirit through a shared rite (no. 6); that the liturgy is the exercise of the priesthood of Christ through sensible signs (no. 7); that the liturgy is salvation history in action by means of the sacrifice and of the sacraments (nos. 2,5,6,48)" (Catella 15).

But the essence of liturgy is far more poetic than these words imply. The Church speaks of the liturgy as the source from which "grace is poured forth upon us as from a fountain" (SC 10), "the outstanding means whereby the faithful may express in their lives and manifest to others the mystery of Christ" (SC 2). It contains symbols that "convey the reality and power of death and resurrection" by which the assembly is drawn into the very life of God (Saliers 20). It provides a radical sense of vision that converts contradiction into congruity by providing "a place of alternative imagination about the structures of the world and therefore a source of hope" (Lathrop 217). Liturgy is about mystery that is new with every moment, "a continual celebration of the mystery of Christ and the spirit, a path that accompanies the everyday experience of the faithful from baptism until the final moment of the paschal passage from death to life" (Cervera 50). Liturgy is expressed in contrasts. "This means that even the cry of pain and the remembrance of suffering and complexity may commingle with the praise and thanks" (Saliers 107). Liturgy forms the identity of the assembly even as it is being formed by the experience of the assembly, existing in a state that "symbolically suspends the flow of time" (Catella 25), creating the space where memory becomes present actuality. "The self-engaging activity of our liturgy not only causes us to remember who we are; it invites us to commit ourselves to a life congruent with our identity. All liturgy is anamnesis" (Collins 79). So by these accounts, liturgy is a source of grace, the expression of the paschal mystery, the symbolic means enabling unity with the life of God, a commingling of contrast, the suspension of time, and a formational element of identity.

These words come closer to defining liturgy but still present an incomplete picture. "The liturgical entity consists ... of the united body of the faithful as such—the church—a body which infinitely outnumbers the mere congregation" (Guardini 19). In liturgy, the sacred is embraced as the assembly, in word, gesture, and sacrifice, enables a most powerful experience. This enables the connection between the kingdom of earth and the kingdom of heaven. "Good liturgical celebration ... lifts us momentarily out of the cesspool of injustice we call home, puts us in the promised and challenging reign of God, where we are treated like we have never been treated anywhere else" (Hovda 364). The earthly order of liturgical ritual is "the ritual access to the salvation-event" (Catella 25) that creates an order of a different kind as it "leads not to the brink of clarity but to the edge of chaos. It deals not with the abolition of ambiguity but with the dark and hidden things of God" (Kavanagh 65). Based on these concepts, a summary of what liturgy is might be "the making present in word, symbol and sacrament of the paschal mystery of Christ so that through its celebration the men and women of today may make a saving encounter with God" (Crichton 17).

That definition has an appealing clarity and simplicity but lacks the depth to describe the reality that is liturgy. Although each of the perspectives above is intriguing, and may capture a certain aspect, the definition remains somewhat elusive. Liturgy is poetry, dance, music, and art in its purest form. Liturgy is life and death, memory and present action, promise, fulfillment, and future. Liturgy is the living identity derived from the experience of the assembly, the people of God, in passionate, intimate dialogue with their creator and redeemer with the inspiration of the Holy Spirit. Liturgy is mystery and understanding that goes beyond words. Liturgy is contrast and unity, humanity and divinity. Liturgy is dynamic, always evolving, always integrated into the paschal mystery. Liturgy impacts every sense; it has a look, feel, sound, smell, and taste, and it connects with the senses of the heart that derive from faith. All of these define liturgy, but in the end the only true and complete definition comes through faith-filled experience. The way to that experience is in responding to the invitation to "taste and see" and in discovering "that the Lord is good" (1Pt 2:3). Conscious, then, of the limitations of words, liturgy may be defined as an active experience of love that by the art of ritual action unifies the human and divine by engaging the paschal mystery, transcending the limits of time and human senses as it invites the community of believers to encounter and embrace the holy. Even at the "last minute," this is the liturgy we seek.

CHAPTER 2

Where to Begin

How to Declare a Liturgical Emergency

In an ideal world, when faced with a crisis requiring a last-minute liturgy, there would be a "liturgical 9-1-1" number you could call. A fully equipped liturgical response team would appear at your doorstep a few minutes later in a rescue vehicle complete with flashing lights in the appropriate liturgical color. Inside would be a complete team of liturgical ministers outfitted with all the liturgical resources you might need, environmental components, vesture, liturgical hardware, ceremonial binders, office supplies, computers, and printers. They would rush in, determine the nature of the liturgical emergency and assess the need. Returning to their vehicle, they would extract the necessary material from their resources and put together worship aids and a presider's book. Returning, they would bring with them all the liturgical elements necessary to engage in liturgy, complete with any necessary ministers.

Sound like fantasy? The flashing lights in the liturgical colors are the only fictional part of the above description. I've never figured out a legal way to put purple flashing lights on my SUV! Seriously, LERT as described in the introduction really exists. We don't actually have a 9-1-1 number, either, but my home phone number (along with the numbers of the rest of the team) seems to work quite well for this. My point is not to suggest that a nationwide system of liturgical 9-1-1 be enacted but rather to demonstrate the simple elements needed to respond quickly to a liturgical need. By avoiding panic and using the many readily available resources, preparing last-minute liturgies is a lot easier than it might appear.

DETERMINE THE NATURE OF THE LITURGICAL EMERGENCY

IS IT A BLESSING, PRAYER, OR SERVICE?

There are three basic types of liturgical emergencies: blessings, prayers, and services. Before going further, determine what type of last-minute liturgy you are attempting to prepare. While this seems obvious, it's not always simple. For example, someone may ask you to bless a new home. On the face of it, this is straightforward: the liturgy type is a blessing; it is a standard form, so grab the *Book of Blessings* and be on your way, right? Blessing a house actually falls into the category of a service because it has a clear structural form and norms for rites of blessing. Picking up the *Book of Blessings* was the right choice; it just was not the complete choice. Reading through the rite of blessing a home you'll find some options in terms of form and components. With a few minutes of extra effort you can prepare a simple liturgy that is prayerful and meets the needs of those who made the request. In a very simple way, we've followed the "rules" of preparing last-minute liturgies by considering the goal (sharing the joy of a new home by invoking God's blessing), using what works (the *Book of Blessings* is a good place to start for almost any "unusual" liturgy), and employing sound liturgical principles of preparation (reading through the ritual *before* actually attempting to lead prayer is unfortunately a relatively uncommon practice). So far, so good. Let's back up just a bit now and consider each of the types of liturgical situations mentioned above.

BLESSINGS

A blessing can range from a very simple action to a relatively complex ritual. A blessing is a way to extend holiness by invoking the presence of God. It can be as simple as blessing a child by tracing the sign of the cross on the forehead or as broad as the "Order of Blessing of Fields and Flocks" (BB 966). All of these can be handled relatively easily with little advance notice. Although we need to be careful about the way we bless and, in some cases, what we bless, this is fairly familiar territory. We have all blessed ourselves and our food. Many of us have blessed our children. We understand that it involves calling on God and trusting in grace.

PRAYERS

This is a rather broad category encompassing the majority of last-minute liturgy requests.

What if you're gathered for a parish meeting and someone looks at you and says, "Will you lead us in prayer?" For some people this request invokes the same level of terror as an impending root canal procedure. I will freely admit that I routinely attempted to avoid these situations (the root canals and the prayer requests). Eventually though, having assumed a role of ministerial leadership, I had to confront this necessity head on (I eventually ran out of teeth, so the root canal bit was no longer an issue). By this time, I had been introduced to the simple formulary for prayer that makes this situation much more manageable. It's the "you, who, through, do" formula. This is described well in Kathleen Hughes's *Lay Presiding: The Art of Leading Prayer*. It is the most basic form of intercessory prayer and it is the structure that is used in most collects in the Catholic tradition. Using this form, we name God (that's the you), we recall what God has done and by what means this has been accomplished (who, through), and based on this we ask God to act on our request. So for example, if asked to lead prayer at the beginning of a meeting during the Easter season, I might come up with something that begins this way: "God of glory, by the wonder of your love you raise Jesus from the dead and invite all to the banquet of eternal life." That's the you, who, and through pieces. Then, "In that same love be present here among us this evening, that our efforts may witness to the wonder of your name." With a little practice and some simple attention to ritual language, this can become second nature.

If you're in an ecumenical situation, you will be pretty safe using a simple invitation to the Lord's Prayer. This is a good way to emphasize our unity rather than the differences in our traditions, but in order for that to work well, the leader should remember to include the doxology. It sounds very odd indeed if all the Catholics in the group become silent after "deliver us from evil" and send the wrong message.

SERVICES

I was asked to prepare a funeral service for a member of the United States Coast Guard Auxiliary. The family of the deceased requested a "nonreligious" service at the funeral home, followed by a burial at sea at a later date. Ordinarily, this would be a fairly straightforward service but in this case there was also a request for a "flower service," which is considered by some to be a nautical tradition. Customarily, this includes the reading of a series of brief texts relating to each of the natural forces that impact on service at sea (fog, waves, wind, stars, ocean spray, and so on). Following each text a flower is placed on the casket. The only trouble was I would not be able to see a copy of this service until I arrived at the funeral home. So far, there was still no need to panic. Armed with excerpts from various military chaplain manuals, including versions of services for most religious traditions, and my copy of the *Liturgy of the Hours* (I thought an adaptation of some of the text from the Office for the Dead might be useful), I arrived at the funeral home. I spent some time with the family and in personal prayer. Twenty minutes before the service was to begin, the officer with the copy of this flower service still had not arrived. This now qualified as a last-minute liturgy! After five more tense minutes passed, the officer with the service arrived. He tossed the copy of the service in my general direction and then ran outside to instruct the military honor guard for the service. Ten minutes before the service was to begin, I started reading through the service, discovering that the entire text contained religious references in almost every other line. Okay, deep breath, still no need to panic! I mentally made a note to alter each phrase containing a religious reference. I whipped out my chaplain's manual, flipped to the nondenominational service section, quickly adapted the form to match the circumstances and placed sticky notes in the places where I would have to flip back and forth between the two services. I inserted the flower service after the eulogy and before the closing. In place of what would be the final collect, I inserted a verse from "Semper Paratus," the Coast Guard "marching song" because I knew that the deceased was proud that he knew all the words. I closed by expressing the desire of all assembled that the deceased might rest in peace and inviting all the uniformed members to come forward and render final honors to the deceased. The result was a dignified service that met the needs of the family, honored the memory of the deceased, and respected the naval tradition.

Following the process I've described for a last-minute liturgy, here's how this service worked:

Determine the nature of the liturgical emergency. Was this to be a blessing, prayer, or service? This was clearly a service and even though the family requested that it be nonreligious, the atmosphere had to be one that was conducive to prayer even though it did not specifically include prayer. The objective here was to meet the needs of all assembled. This was accomplished relatively simply by using existing resources. Of course, having familiarity with these resources (and having them readily at hand) was a crucial element.

Consider the goal. The goal in this situation was clear: to lead a service that would honor the dead and bring comfort to the family and all the bereaved and to keep with the tradition of the Coast Guard. When the goal is this clear-cut, the entire process is simplified.

Don't panic. This was a challenge. Knowing that I had to lead a service containing at least one element with which I was unfamiliar made me uncomfortable and the ten-minute time frame for preparation was certainly less than optimal. Here's where a good working knowledge of a wide range of ritual and ritual language comes to the rescue. Having resources on hand as a backup also relieved some of the pressure. I knew that even if the officer with the flower service failed to arrive, I had enough ritual elements in my chaplain manual and *Liturgy of the Hours* to lead a brief service that would suffice. Always having a backup plan is a big part of taking the stress out of the process. Note that I did not carry with me the *Rite of Christian Burial*. Usually this is a good backup for any type of memorial service because it contains sufficient variety in text to be used (sometimes with adaptation) for most circumstances. In this case, since the family had specifically requested a nonreligious service, I did not want to take the chance of my not being able to reword the text quickly enough. The result could have been damaging to the family.

If you are a person of faith and you are asked to lead a nonreligious service, don't make the mistake of not praying! You do yourself (and your God) dishonor by this. Pray before you begin, *pray while you are leading the service,* and pray when you conclude. Although you will not be praying aloud during the service, maintain an awareness of God's presence in you and through you. If you are asked to lead a service in a tradition other than your own, condescension should not be part of your response. All people are made in the image and likeness of God and we are called to honor the God present in all. Respect their customs and traditions and look carefully to see where the Spirit is moving.

Use what works. The services in the chaplain manuals of any of the armed forces have been tested by time and tradition. With just a bit of creative input and modification of the text to match the circumstances, a service was constructed that worked. No need to try to build a service when one already existed.

Use a team approach to preparation. In this case, I focused my energy and attention on presiding and left the "military" parts of the service to those leading the honor guard and commanding the attending uniformed members. I relied on the staff of the funeral home to prepare the space in accordance with military tradition. Had I attempted to do all of this myself, the service would have suffered.

Use sound liturgical principles. This may seem odd, given that this was intended to be a nonreligious service, but liturgical principles focus on the participation of the assembly and on preparing an environment where God may be encountered. Following those principles, the service I prepared involved many persons in the process (fourteen were involved in the flower service, for example). Although there was no specific prayer in this particular service, I used posture, gesture, silence, and poetically crafted words to enable an experience of God's presence.

Months later, I received a request from a family who desired a Catholic service. I followed essentially the same process, except that I used the *Order of Christian Funerals* as the basic resource and used the ritual elements of a wake service rather than the nonreligious elements of the previous service.

Now a word about adaptation. Last-minute liturgies frequently, but not always, require some degree of adaptation. The *Book of Blessings* (GI IV, 32) says, "With a view to the particular circumstances and taking into account the wishes of the faithful, the celebrant or minister is to make full use of the options authorized in the various rites, but also is to maintain the structure of the celebration and is not to mix up the order of the principal parts." If you are using, for example, one of the blessings out of the *Book of Blessings* in the circumstance for which it was intended (using the "Blessing of a New Home" to bless a new home), very little should be altered from the rite as it is laid out. Different psalms and readings may be selected, for example, or the intercessions might be composed for this particular situation, but the parts should all be retained. Omitting the blessing at the end would render the rest of the ritual useless. Putting the blessing at the beginning dishonors the place of the word of God in any celebration of blessing. Even if you have to do major reconstructive surgery on a blessing to make it fit the circumstance, the structure should be retained. I once was asked to construct a blessing prayer for a new elevator in a parish church. The community had invited their archbishop to preside at the first Mass after a restoration of their worship space (including the construction of the elevator) had been completed. The pastor had asked that he bless the elevator during the Mass, so I was left with the task of creating a blessing prayer for an elevator during Mass. I opted to combine elements of "Blessings of Objects That Are Designed or Erected for Use in Churches ..." with elements of the "Order for the Blessing of the Various Means of Transportation." Ordinarily blessing of vehicles would not take place during a Mass but since this was actually part of the church building and was intended to facilitate worship, I used the former blessing structure. The point I'm trying to make here is that we don't ordinarily use a blessing designed for use outside of Mass within a eucharistic liturgy. The master of ceremonies for the archbishop took great delight in asking me silly questions such as "Which deacon accompanies the archbishop for the blessing of the elevator? Would that be the deacon of the word or the deacon of the Eucharist?" People like to torture liturgists. I think that's the reason many of us have earned the reputation peculiar to liturgists.

WHY BEING PREPARED FOR LITURGICAL EMERGENCIES IS EASIER THAN IT SEEMS

Often the first response to a request for a prayer or service on short notice is simple panic. This is particularly true for folks who are not accustomed to preparing liturgy, public prayer, or presiding. While approaching any type of prayer should evoke humble respect, there is no need to panic. The best way to avoid panic, of course, is to be prepared. I mentioned in the introduction that I work closely with the

U.S. Coast Guard. Their motto is "Semper Paratus," which loosely translated means "Always Ready." That's a good way to avoid being unprepared. Being always ready for liturgy is a little bit like taking a first aid course and then keeping a first aid kit around just in case you need it. Studying the basics of liturgical principles and having a reasonable library of resources on hand is the best preparation for liturgical emergencies. Certainly the more you engage in the work of liturgy the better you will become. To some extent preparing liturgy is a skill like any other; practice makes perfect. But even without a great deal of knowledge and with a limited bookshelf, it's not hard to prepare reasonable liturgies, so long as you remember not to panic. After all, God's in control. Whenever we let go and let God, the response is one of faith.

CHAPTER 3

RESOURCES AND HOW TO USE
THEM AT THE LAST MINUTE

One of my favorite lines in my liturgical career has been "I don't make this stuff up!" This applies to liturgical law, guidelines, prayers, texts, posture, gesture, and a whole list of other things. It doesn't mean that I'm not creative. It doesn't mean that I am such a rigid rubricist that I hold the letter of the law above all else. It doesn't mean that I value liturgy over people, nor doctrine over spontaneous prayer. It means that I respect the value of ritual, not for its own sake but for the connection it makes through eternity (in both directions) and for the identity that it preserves. I respect the law of liturgy, not just because it is law but because it represents the vision of a people committed to living in word and worship all that the Gospel demands of them. I treasure the words of the church because so many of them were painstakingly crafted by people truly inspired by the Holy Spirit. These words are poetic and though it is sometimes necessary to adapt or modify them, I do so with great care for they are a fragile treasure. Similarly, posture and gesture require close attention for they often communicate far more than our words or ritual dialogue. The point here is to avoid "making stuff up" whenever possible. Using the available resources and adapting them as necessary is easier and generally more appropriate than trying to create a liturgy out of nothing.

Having said all that, I have to confess to one weakness in my approach. When I know what I'm looking for and I have a clear idea of where to find it, my process of locating and adapting (if necessary) the appropriate ritual is logical and proceeds in an orderly fashion. When I'm not certain exactly what I need, I take every resource that I have that I think might be of use and pile it up on the floor in my living room (or if it's really urgent, it gets packed up in the LERT vehicle) and bounce back and forth between books until I find a combination that works. Even though this is not the most orderly way in which to proceed, it still is not random. Once I pick a starting point, the texts will remind me of where else to look. In general, the best starting point is a ritual book.

THE BOOK OF BLESSINGS

First on my list of useful liturgical resources is definitely the *Book of Blessings* (Collegeville, Minn.: The Liturgical Press, 1989). The list of objects, persons, and situations that can be blessed using the prayers in this book is quite extensive. It contains many forms for blessing of persons — blessing of a family, blessing on the anniversary of marriage, blessing of baptized children, blessing of an engaged couple, blessing of a person suffering from addiction, blessing of students and teachers, blessing of ecumenical groups, blessing for those gathered at a meeting, to name just a few. The *Book of Blessings* also has blessings related to buildings, for objects for use in churches or in popular devotions, seasonal blessings, blessings for various means of transportation, and my personal favorite, the blessing of technical installations or equipment. The last is my personal favorite because I rely heavily on technology in my ministry and have often been tempted to perform an exorcism on some of my equipment! (Sometimes the only way to explain the erratic behavior of computer networks is to believe in possession by demons.) In all seriousness, the scope of the prayers contained in this book is extensive and can be adapted to fit almost any situation in which a blessing is needed. If you need to do a quick prayer or blessing of the "garden variety," the *Book of Blessings* is the place to start.

Here's a typical example: At 7:15 P.M. your frantic pastor appears in your office. So far, this is nothing out of the ordinary. He says that it is his turn to give the opening prayer for the town council this month, and they are meeting at 7:30. He asks if you could possibly run over and give a quick blessing because he has been called away for an emergency. You agree and ask for the text he's prepared. He looks at you as if you have three horns growing out of your head and growls, "Oh, just make something up." Here's where the *Book of Blessings* comes in. You flip to the table of contents, find chapter 6, "Orders for the Blessing of Those Gathered at a Meeting," and turn to it. Since you're uncertain which religious traditions might be represented at this meeting, you decide against the "Blessing of Those Gathered at a Meeting," which assumes a Catholic gathering, or the Christian-oriented "Blessing for Ecumenical Groups." Section III, "Prayers for Interfaith Gatherings," looks like it would work. An adaptation for a meeting of civil leaders might sound something like this:

> God of all creation,
> your presence gives us courage.
> You have called these your servants together this evening
> to work together for the good of our community.

Grant them your wisdom

that they may faithfully serve those who place their trust in them.

Strengthen them that their good work may find its end in you.

Grant them vision that in the days to come their labor may bear great
fruit.

Remain with them that all they do may be with your blessing.

Amen.

This is an adaptation written with very broad strokes based on the
concepts, rather than the words and structure contained in the BB. In
the scenario that I described above, with only fifteen minutes to
prepare, I would probably choose to use the BB as written or perhaps
with a few modifications at the moment. All it would take for a
last-minute liturgy in this case would be to find the right page in the
BB, set the ribbon there, and be on your way. The key to this and every
other response to the unexpected is being able to use the tools at hand.

Catholic Household Blessings & Prayers

Another useful but underutilized tool is *Catholic Household Blessings &
Prayers*. I haven't seen this handy little book in too many households,
but it's on the bookshelf of every liturgy coordinator I know. The *Book
of Blessings* is designed for the moments of the life of the community,
and CHBP was created for every moment in the life of the family at
home. They went a bit overboard with the number of events they chose
to bless but this works in our favor. If you need a prayer or blessing for
something and you can't quite find a parallel in BB, try CHBP. Chances
are that you'll have to adapt it to fit your need, but you'll have a solid

starting foundation from which to build. There is literally a prayer for every minute of the day, in every liturgical season, from waking in the morning, through washing and dressing, eating and drinking, working, studying, almsgiving, coming home, at table, after meals, and at bedside. The prayers for "various times and places" includes, for example, prayers for welcoming guests, leaving on a journey, and leaving home for school, and blessings of the work of an artist, objects for use or entertainment, and objects for prayer and devotion, just to name a few. At the end of this extensive list is a generic blessing "to be used in various circumstances" for use in the unlikely event that you find yourself in a situation not covered by all the other prayers.

Here's an example of how this might happen. In response to a request from some local catechists, I designed an activity for children soon to celebrate first communion and their parents. It involved prayer, an opportunity for the children to teach their parents what they had learned, and a chance for families to work together to decorate a child-sized communion cup that would be used as a focus for family prayer in final days of preparation for first communion. I published an article describing the event (see *Ministry & Liturgy* Dec. 2001 p.12–14) and was surprised at the interest it generated.

At one point, the director of religious education in the parish where I was working at the time cornered me and declared a liturgical emergency. She had scheduled this first communion activity as a retreat experience but she didn't realize that not all the elements that would be needed for the day as she had prepared it were included in my outline. She wanted prayers to fit her version and she needed them right away so that she could review them with her catechetical team. The way I had designed it, the event began with a simple greeting and prayer. The prayer that I recommended for that was an adaptation of the "Blessing Before First Communion" from *Catholic Household Blessing & Prayers* (Blessings During Childhood). For the other moments in that activity, I recommended adaptations of other existing prayers. For the blessing of the cups after their families had decorated them, I suggested an adaptation of the "Order for the Blessing of a Chalice and Paten" (BB 1381), crafting the text carefully so that there would be no confusion about the nature of this blessing. The closing prayer was taken from Eucharistic Prayer III for Masses with Children, again with some adaptation. With that in hand, another liturgical crisis was averted. This situation was slightly more challenging than some because the nature of the prayer was somewhat out of the ordinary and the assembly consisted of a mixed group of people. These prayers had to be sculpted in a way that they would be appropriate for adults as well as children. The structure of the day did not follow an ordinary liturgical pattern, so care was taken to form prayer that would lend a sense of gathering and welcome, an experience of praise and blessing, and a feeling of sending forth. Using these two books of blessing was not enough. A ritual book with more concrete structure was needed.

THE SACRAMENTARY

The sacramentary is the primary reference for ritual structure; however, it's not used as a reference as often as it should. One of the best ways to be prepared for any liturgical event is to learn to speak the language of liturgy, and the sacramentary is the textbook for the course. Considerations of translation and gender inclusivity aside, this book speaks the language of a love so powerful that even death is no match for it. Here are the gestures, postures, and movements we use when we gather to celebrate our communal sacramental moments. Here are the words we use to communicate in ritual dialogue with one another and with our God. I am an advocate of adaptation, of carefully crafting the ritual experience of a community to be unique while still firmly rooted in the universal prayer of the church. I have spent a lifetime making the language of liturgy the way of my own life. I can weave images into a seamless garment of poetic text when the Holy Spirit is kind enough to break through my writer's block. But I am humble enough to know that my own words, gesture, and posture are inadequate when it comes to communal prayer. In the same way, when our country found itself suddenly and inexplicably attacked by an unseen and unknown enemy, the words I was called to pray aloud were first the words of the church and not my own.

> "God our Father,
> maker and lover of peace,
> to know you is to live,
> and to serve you is to reign.
> All our faith is in your saving help;
> protect us from men of violence
> and keep us safe from weapons of hate"
> (Opening Prayer, Masses for Various Needs and Occasions: 23. In Time of War or Civil Disturbance).

Later, when we realized that we were only strong as a nation, as a world, when we put aside our divisions, we prayed:

> "Father, all-powerful and ever-living God,
> we praise and thank you through Jesus Christ our Lord
> for your presence and action in the world.

In the midst of conflict and division,

we know it is you

who turn our minds to thoughts of peace.

Your Spirit changes our hearts:

enemies begin to speak to one another,

those who were estranged join hands in friendship,

and nations seek the way of peace together.

Your Spirit is at work

when understanding puts an end to strife,

when hatred is quenched by mercy,

and vengeance gives way to forgiveness"

(Eucharistic Prayer for Masses of Reconciliation II).

I'm not suggesting that the prayers in the sacramentary should be used verbatim as a general response for other liturgical needs. The opening prayers, the prayers over the gifts, and the prayers after communion are each crafted for a specific ritual moment, but by studying the phrasing, the cadence, and the general flow of the language, it's possible to begin building a vocabulary of worship. The rubrics in the sacramentary are dreaded by some, are pointed to as divine law by others, and should be neither. Rather, they are the structure around which dialogue takes place. As humans, we find comfort in predictable behavior, and we define social rules so that we can be comfortable with each other. This is especially true when the unexpected happens. When we act in a predictable way in the face of the unexpected, we regain some control and can begin the process of re-forming our corporate identity. That is the gift that the sacramentary gives us. It teaches us the basics of how to speak and act when we come together to pray. If the sacramentary is the "grammar" of the language of liturgy, some of the other ritual books form the "conversation" and "etiquette" of liturgy.

THE LITURGY OF THE HOURS

If the sacramentary is the "primer" of liturgical word and action, the Liturgy of the Hours is the advanced work. Without a doubt, the Liturgy of the Hours is the most underused liturgical treasure of the church. In it, the language of liturgy is spoken fluently, the richness of the psalms explored, and poetic prayer expressed. If you are responsible for preparing any form of prayer in your community, the *Liturgy of the Hours* belongs on your bookshelf. Skip the abbreviated one-volume *Christian Prayer* and go for the four-volume seasonal set. It's worth the additional expense to have all of the texts for each of the seasons of the liturgical year. The *Liturgy of the Hours* contains psalms, prayers, readings (both scriptural and non-biblical), and intercessions for the various liturgical hours of each day. People often make fun of the amount of gear that I carry around with me — to work as a scientist, to church as a liturgist, and in my seabag. The truth is that I'm usually prepared for whatever happens, and I can generally fix whatever goes wrong. I always carry duct tape; when all else fails, I can do a lot with duct tape. The *Liturgy of the Hours* is the duct tape of my liturgical tool kit. It's both a good starting point and a good ending point. Obviously, it's the right tool when preparing Morning Prayer or Evening Prayer, but its usefulness extends way beyond that. Suppose, for example, your parish environment committee is in church on Christmas Eve morning, preparing to decorate the church for the Christmas celebrations, and unexpectedly they ask if you would lead them in prayer once everyone has arrived. Here's how you can adapt these prayers for a particular use. If you grab volume one of the *Liturgy of the Hours*, flip to December 24th Morning Prayer and jump to the intercessions, you'll find a brief section of prayer almost tailor-made for this moment. Begin with a signing and greeting (careful with the form of the greeting if you're a layperson—more on that later), and continue with the invitation to prayer: "To Jesus Christ, our Redeemer, who will come again in glory with great power, let us make our humble prayer, as we pray: Come, Lord Jesus!" By constructing the invitation to prayer this way, those gathered will respond to each intercession with that response. Interaction is, of course, crucial to good liturgy. Continue with each of the intercessions, including an invitation for any particular needs for which the group might pray. If you recraft the final intercession in this way, "We long for the grace of your coming. Console us with the gift of your own divine life as we pray in the words you gave us … Our Father …," you can make a smooth transition into the Lord's Prayer. Again, this allows for active participation. You can conclude with the proper closing prayer of that day, which has an appropriate pivotal Advent into Christmas flavor: "Come Lord Jesus, do not delay; give new courage to your people who trust in your love. By your coming, raise us to the joy of your kingdom, where you live and reign…." If this were an actual Morning Prayer, it would conclude with the proper blessing (May almighty God bless us …) but it's not necessary in this case. So here you have a simple, elegant, appropriate prayer connected to the universal prayer of the church that suited a particular need with minimal adaptation. That's a hard combination to beat! Using the Hours in this way is just the tip of the iceberg. Exploring this liturgical form reveals the complexity of beauty of the psalter, the liturgical collection of psalms. There is a psalm text, I believe, for every human emotion and every human condition. Meant to be sung, when committed to memory, the psalms form a tapestry of prayer that is both comforting and challenging. I often wonder why we teach our children liturgical and devotional prayers such as the Lord's Prayer and the Hail Mary but rarely teach them psalmody. My own background is such that I have learned musical settings of most of the psalter, and those are the words and melodies that spring to my mind and lips in times of trouble and joy. For example, I once found myself in a life-threatening situation along with two other Catholics and a Jewish friend. What came to my mind was Psalm 91, in something of an amalgam of translations formed of the many settings I've prayed over the years. From Dan Schutte's "Blest Be the Lord" (New Dawn, 1976), Michael Joncas's "On Eagle's Wings" (New Dawn, 1979), and Marty Haugen's "Be With Me" (GIA, 1980) of my early years in ministry along with later experiences of chant and other forms, the sound of the text resonated clearly within me. I could easily have sung any one of those renditions or recited the words, but more importantly, the essence of that prayer of protection came readily and immediately to mind. I found that my Jewish friend was praying the same psalm, though in somewhat different words. Although the words that I recalled were not a literal translation, the sense and meaning was clear enough. As people who dwell by faith in the secret places of Elyon, who trust in Yahweh, and who know the safety of the shadow of Shaddai, he and I were able to pray together free from the fear of the terrors of that night with that psalm as our common ground.

> No evil shall befall you, no pain come near,
> for the angels stand close by your side,
> guarding you always and bearing you gently, watching over your life.

Those who cling to the Lord live secure in God's love,
lifted high, those who trust in God's name,
call on the Lord, who will never forsake you.
God will bring you salvation and joy.

My Catholic friends were struggling. For one, all that came to mind was a table blessing, grace; for the other, the Hail Mary. I imagine that the Hail Mary brought some comfort, for it did seem that we were "at the hour of our death," but I don't imagine that the prayers of blessing before a meal were of much help for my other friend. While it is certainly true that the desire to pray is more important than the words of prayer, appropriate words have the potential to change us. Many of those words can be found in the *Liturgy of the Hours* if you know where to look.

Ordo

The ordo is one way to find out where to look when using any of the liturgical resources. The long form of its title is "The Order of Prayer in the Liturgy of the Hours and Celebration of the Eucharist" and it is published new each liturgical year by a number of agencies. There you can search by the calendar date and see the liturgical season, the liturgical day, the color of vesture, the readings for the Mass of the day, the psalm cycle for the Hours of the day, along with various options for celebrations. There are also pastoral notes making recommendations for various prayers and blessings that might be used on a particular liturgical day. The norms for liturgical seasons are described briefly here. It's something of a pocket-guide to the liturgy, although the abbreviations and language take a little while to process and translate.

These days, any gadget that requires any sort of setup usually comes with two sets of instructions. One is usually a "quick setup" giving the bare minimum of how to get all the parts together in the right configuration as quickly as possible. The second set, a "detailed setup," is a more in-depth description with an explanation of all the options and features that require a little more time and patience to put to use. Think of the ordo as the "quick setup" and the introductory documents to the liturgical sources as the "detailed setup."

LECTIONARY

It may seem strange to use the lectionary as a source of scriptural text when there are so many other translations and formats available. Certainly there will be times when a particular translation or style will be better suited than the lectionary for a particular purpose. But as a resource for liturgy in general, the lectionary is my first choice because it sorts text by season and celebration and combines text in a way that is both familiar and manageable. If you're looking for a passage related to a particular type of event and your knowledge of Scripture is not strong, you have a much better chance of finding what you need in the lectionary than you do by randomly searching through a Bible. For example, if you need a reading that speaks of hope in the face of adversity, likely the best place to look would be among the prophetic readings for the Sundays of Advent. Consider the Third Sunday of Advent Year A, Isaiah 35:1–6a,10:

> The desert and the parched land will exult;
>> the steppe will rejoice and bloom.
> They will bloom with abundant flowers,

and rejoice with joyful song.
The glory of Lebanon will be given to them,
    the splendor of Carmel and Sharon;
they will see the glory of the LORD,
    the splendor of our God.
Strengthen the hands that are feeble,
    make firm the knees that are weak,
say to those whose hearts are frightened:
    Be strong, fear not!
Here is your God,
    he comes with vindication;
with divine recompense
    he comes to save you.
Then will the eyes of the blind be opened,
    the ears of the deaf be cleared;
then will the lame leap like a stag,
    then the tongue of the mute will sing.

Those whom the LORD has ransomed will return
    and enter Zion singing,
    crowned with everlasting joy;
they will meet with joy and gladness,
    sorrow and mourning will flee.

The lectionary breaks this text into manageable pieces; using the entire length of Isaiah 35 would be awkward. Here the powerful message of hope is articulated clearly. It's easy to apply the same principle to other liturgical seasons. Suppose you need a reading that reflects unconditional love. The Lenten readings are the clear choice for this.

Romans 5:1–2,5–8, the second reading for the Third Sunday of Lent Year A is a good example of this:

> Brothers and sisters:
>> Since we have been justified by faith,
>> we have peace with God through our Lord Jesus Christ,
>> through whom we have gained access by faith
>> to this grace in which we stand,
>> and we boast in hope of the glory of God.
>
> And hope does not disappoint,
>> because the love of God has been poured out into our
>>> hearts
>> through the Holy Spirit who has been given to us.
> For Christ, while we were still helpless,
>> died at the appointed time for the ungodly.
> Indeed, only with difficulty does one die for a just person,
>> though perhaps for a good person one might even find
>>> courage to die.
> But God proves his love for us
>> in that while we were still sinners Christ died for us.

The section that is left out in this reading (Romans 5:4) is the part that tends to make folks' heads spin:

> Not only that, but we even boast of our afflictions,
>> knowing that affliction produces endurance,
>> and endurance, proven character,
>> and proven character, hope ….

This is an important piece and certainly worthy of reflection, but it is extremely hard to follow in proclaimed form. This is the strength of the lectionary, for the texts are intended specifically for proclamation. Even if you can't find the perfect reading in the lectionary, chances are you will at least come away from it with an idea of where to find a fuller reading or a related text. Speaking of related texts, be careful how you use Scripture texts. If you are preparing a defined liturgy, such as Evening Prayer or a Mass for some special occasion, stick to the ritual book designated for that purpose. This will ensure that you're using the correct translation and an approved selection for the liturgy in question. If, on the other hand, you're preparing a service that is not liturgical, you have much more flexibility regarding both prayer and Scripture texts. An outstanding source of scriptural material that is either absent from the lectionary or differs significantly in translation is *Remembering the Women: Women's Stories from Scripture for Sundays and Festivals.*

CONCORDANCE

Sometimes you'll find that there's a text that you want or need, but you're not sure what the exact Scripture citation is for it. I frequently have this problem because, despite having completed a reasonable amount of coursework in Scripture, the way I'm most likely to recall scriptural text is by a musical setting of that text that I have learned. Sometimes that method works well. For example I once learned a setting of the Passion text from John's Gospel. That setting used a literal liturgical translation of the text, so when I call the melody to mind, the text that goes with it is true to the translation. More often, though, if I recall the words of some setting, those words are slightly different than the actual translation. There's nothing wrong with that, so long as I don't make the mistake of deliberately using those texts verbatim as proclaimed word at liturgy. When I'm reaching for a text, I make good use of an electronic concordance, although the traditional bound type works well also. I like the electronic version because it saves time when I'm putting together a liturgy quickly. I can type in, for example, a combination of words that I believe to be in the text that I want, and it displays all the text where that combination of words is found. Since I use a NAB concordance, I can use the text directly. Alternatively, once I've found the text I want, I can look the citation up in the lectionary index to find where it appears. Then, if available, I can use the lectionary or Book of the Gospels, as appropriate, for proclamation, which is generally preferable to any other resource.

MUSIC RESOURCES AND LITURGICAL INDICES

Sometimes I just need to work backwards from the music that I recall to the scriptural text that I want. If the text used in the musical setting doesn't exactly match the scriptural text, this can sometimes be a problem when using the concordance, but fortunately many of the music worship aids currently in use have outstanding indices. With respect to the Psalm 91 example I used above, if I could remember the song, "Be With Me," but I couldn't recall which psalm this was, I could pick up a hymnal (GIA's *Gather Comprehensive* in this case, as I knew that the song was in that resource) and look up the song. Once I've found the song, I'll have the text to which it refers, for it's referenced at the end of the song. Happily, it works the other way as well. If I needed a setting for Psalm 91, I could look that up in the scriptural index and find all the settings in that resource for Psalm 91. This is an easy, uncomplicated example. A more challenging example would be needing music for a particular type of service or one with a particular need. Fortunately, many of the music resources include a topical index with categories such as courage, compassion, and fear, which are of great help at the last minute when dealing with such intense emotions. In addition, in some of these resources there is a liturgical index, an index of hymns by the familiar first line, and an index by composer. A word of caution is merited here, though. As good as the resources are and as wonderful as the index compilation of each may be, there is simply no substitute for a good pastoral musician (the operative word there being "pastoral"). Always engage the talents of those people first. If they are unavailable, then by all means make use of the books. An intimate knowledge of liturgical music and a sensitivity to sung prayer are not qualities to be taken lightly. However, this does not mean that you should have fear of selecting music for a last-minute liturgy.

There are some general principles for selecting music for liturgy in general and last-minute liturgies in particular. For any liturgy, choose music that is worthy of use in prayer. Popular music, while it may seem to suit the occasion, rarely has enough depth to do justice to worship. Avoid the temptation of picking your favorite liturgical music simply because you like it. If it doesn't fit, it will be meaningless. At the other extreme, don't exhaust yourself trying to find the perfect fit for every liturgy. Sometimes the perfect song just doesn't exist; more often, the connection between sung prayer and ritual evolves in the moment. Let God do the work there.

When dealing with the unexpected, your resources may be limited and you may be trying to minister to an assembly unaccustomed to worshiping together. Here you will want to use the best music that is familiar to all. If you have someone who is able to lead song, you can strengthen the unity of the assembly by using selections having simple, easy to learn antiphons. Keep the music simple, familiar, and inclusive. It is better not to include a song than to use one that excludes some portion of the assembly.

OTHER RITUAL BOOKS

In addition to the sacramentary and the lectionary, other ritual books are solid resources for preparing a variety of liturgies. Despite the title, *The Order of Christian Funerals* (the full version) contains prayer and Scripture texts for each of the moments surrounding death. Although familiar to priest presiders, this ritual book is less well known among lay leaders of prayer, who may be more accustomed to versions containing only the vigil rites. In addition to the funeral liturgy, it contains the vigil for the deceased, the prayers after death, the gathering in the presence of the body, the transfer of the body to the church of the place of committal, and the rite of committal. Beyond that, it contains prayers and Scripture selections for times when we often have no words that are up to the task. The "Rite of Final Commendation for an Infant," "Funerals for Baptized Children," and "Funerals for Children Who Died Before Baptism" are tailored for situations that we all find difficult. Similarly, the "Prayers and Texts in Particular Circumstances" section includes prayers for those who died by suicide or by violence. When confronted with a need for any sort of service related to a death, head for this ritual book first. Next to the *Book of Blessings*, it is the book that I use most frequently. It seems that there is an increasing need for end-of-life rituals and a decreasing number of persons willing and able to lead or facilitate these rites.

Pastoral Care of the Sick is one of the more familiar ritual books. It gets enough use on a regular basis to have earned a permanent home in my car. It is easily adaptable for a variety of situations, although the layout is somewhat awkward. Despite the fact that it includes complete versions of pastoral visits to the sick, communion of the sick, anointing, viaticum, and rites for emergencies, this ritual is still somewhat underutilized. Although bringing communion to the sick is a relatively common event, including the ritual elements proper to this event is uncommon. Here's where a prayerful response to the unexpected is relatively easy. If asked to bring communion to a person who is homebound or in the hospital, the ritual contains just about everything you will need. There really is no excuse for the all-too-frequent occurrence when a communion minister arrives at the bedside, says hello, perhaps exchanges pleasantries, whips out a host, administers communion, perhaps says the Lord's Prayer, and departs. If this sounds disrespectful to the real presence in all its manifestations, it is. The ritual exists to transform what could be a social visit (at best) or an impersonal interaction (at worst) into a sacred moment. Mere words and actions can't do this, but they help to create an atmosphere and an environment in which a sacramental encounter can take place.

Although not a recognized ritual book itself, *A Ritual for Laypersons* is a handy collection of ritual prayer extracted from *Holy Communion and the Worship of Eucharist Outside of Mass, Pastoral Care of the Sick: Rites of Anointing and Viaticum* and *The Order of Christian Funerals,* which were constructed using the formularies for lay presiders.

OLD AND ODD BOOKS

I collect books. Actually, I collect old liturgical books, old missals, and prayer books and books about liturgy. It's a very odd collection, but when I'm called on to construct something of an odd prayer, that's where I turn. I was once asked to create a series of prayers for use on a retreat by men who were discerning a vocation to the priesthood. It sounded relatively simple, and I agreed. At virtually the last minute, I received an important "bit" of information: These men were of varied backgrounds, all spoke little English, and most were relatively new to Christianity. I had spent a good deal of time working on layers of imagery and abstract wording with the intent of leaving enough "space" in these reflections to give these earnest young men some spiritual breathing room. Clearly, because of their limited English language skills, my efforts would have the opposite effect. The words I had chosen would likely be confusing and frustrating for them. I put aside the work that I'd completed (and filed it away for future use, of course!) and started over. This time I began with an antique version of the *St. Joseph's Children's Missal.* I adapted some of those prayers to fit the context and constructed reflections that were clear in language. I'll admit that it was a challenge for me to be stripped to such basic language, but the result was elegant in its simplicity. I learned a lesson in humility and those young men were gifted with a prayer experience that was far more profound than what I would have constructed if left to my own devices.

Sometimes it's helpful to include language from another faith tradition when preparing a service of some sort. This can be tricky when working in an interfaith environment, but if done well, it can foster a sense of inclusivity that might be otherwise impossible. Be careful with this. Do not incorporate elements of other faith traditions into an existing liturgical celebration unless there are local norms permitting this. To "mix and match" the language of different traditions does injury to all. On the other hand, if you are working with a group that is preparing an ecumenical or interfaith service of some sort, to exclude the words of one tradition in favor of another is inappropriate. This can be a very fine line. I have in my collection *Prayers for All People* by Mary Ford-Grabowsky, which has a wide variety of prayers from numerous traditions including Judaism, Islam, Hinduism, Buddhism, Celtic, Mayan, and Native American. Of course it must be used with care, but it is interesting to see how different cultures approach different aspects of the human condition. I have copies of the 1945 and 1977 editions of the *Episcopal Book of Common Prayer*, which I've found to be very useful for the extensive orders of prayer and careful phrasing found there. Another good source of prayer texts linked to seasons is *Prayers for Sundays and Seasons*. Old missals, and old and new hymnals are also good sources of useful texts. You may have to do some adaptation, but sometimes all you need is one good idea or a nudge in the right direction to develop text that is worthy of use in prayer.

WEB RESOURCES

This is an exciting and sometimes dangerous resource. It's exciting because it has the potential to save an enormous amount of time, which can be a lifesaver at the last minute. It's dangerous because it is easy to violate a copyright by mistake or to use material that may be inaccurate or incomplete. But used with discretion and care, the resources of the internet can be invaluable. A very simple example would be how the use of e-mail allows for the sharing of talent and material over distances that would be difficult or impossible otherwise. I had a request from a colleague who found herself putting together a memorial service at the last minute. She called me because there was a certain dialogue reading that I had used effectively in a similar situation. I was able to e-mail her the entire service, complete with worship aids, in a matter of minutes. She was then able to edit the material, customize it to her specific needs, and use it that very evening. This would have been impossible by any other method. We were on opposite ends of the country. Any sort of surface delivery would have been too late. Faxing would have left her with a copy of mediocre quality that was not editable, and the worship aid would have had to have been entirely reconstructed. This of course is the easiest situation, one in which you know exactly what you're looking for and whom to ask to get it. Situations are rarely that easy.

A more complicated example is related to a military memorial service at which I presided in July 2002, honoring the fallen members of a U.S. Coast Guard Auxiliary flotilla throughout its history. Although the service had been planned well in advance, this was an unexpected event for me, as I did not know I was expected to prepare the service until very shortly before the date. This is a case in which the web saved me. First I searched to find the general form of a memorial at sea, which I thought I could use as a very loose framework around which to construct this service. I found that service on the U.S. Navy chaplain's website, requested and received permission to use the text in my own service. So far, so good. Based on what I had learned, I decided that the service would have the form of a greeting with brief introductory comments, followed by a call to attention and the national anthem, a call to prayer, an introduction to and reading of the names of the deceased by the flotilla commander, a committal, benediction, and taps. Constructing the greeting was simple, for at that time, emotions were still high following the attacks of September 11, 2001, and this flotilla had lost one of its own that year. The next part, the national anthem, was a little more difficult. I knew we had a bugler for taps at the end, but I expected to need a recording of the national anthem (sometimes you just can't avoid using recorded music, though I try to avoid it at all costs). The web provided a simple solution. I went online and searched for "Star Spangled Banner." I found a commercial site that had "Salute to the Services: The Military Band" for sale. Included on that CD was the national anthem, taps, and "Semper Paratus," the Coast Guard hymn. Knowing that I would, at some point in time, need all of those, I ordered the CD. But that alone would not have met my needs, as it would be two or three days before I would receive the CD. Thankfully, there were sample tracks on the site, including "The Star Spangled Banner" which I downloaded and burned onto a CD. There's an important point to be made here. Since I had purchased the CD, it was not a violation of copyright law to use the track that I downloaded. On the other hand, it would be unethical to download and use the music without paying for it. This is true of any copyrighted material you may find on the web, but it is of particular concern for graphics and music. Just because you can download it does not make it yours.

Constructing the rest of the service was relatively simple: extracting and adapting the appropriate elements from the memorial at sea and replacing the Navy prayer with the Coast Guard prayer. Again, I was able to find the Coast Guard prayer online. Once I had the service put together and polished, I converted it to a portable document format and e-mailed it to the flotilla commander and the detail commander of the color guard so that they would have a chance to review their parts in the service ahead of time.

This is a very specific example of how to use electronic resources, but the possibilities out there are many; they are too variable and too numerous to list here. There are websites listing the liturgical calendar for the next five years. That's helpful when you want to find out when Christmas next falls on Monday, the most dreaded event of liturgists, so you can plan to be on vacation then. There are websites that display Scripture citations in a variety of different translations for comparison and selection. There are liturgy planning websites, and music planning websites, all of which can be extraordinarily helpful in a pinch. The best thing to do is to browse these sites when you're not under a tight deadline so that when the time comes to crank out a service at the last minute you have some idea where to look. One huge word of caution, though. Never rely on the web as your primary resource. If you do, you can bet that at the precise moment you need it the most, your server will go down, there will be a power failure, or some other event will prevent your access to the site you need.

If you have a handheld computer, take advantage of its portability and power and install an electronic Bible or two, and any files or resources you use frequently. My electronic Bible has come to my rescue on many an occasion when I was taken completely by surprise by a liturgical need. Having the liturgical calendar installed is of great help, also.

ANYTHING YOU'VE EVER USED BEFORE

I'm a liturgical pack rat. I prepared my first liturgy on an IBM Selectric typewriter. I still have copies of that, for purely nostalgic reasons. I moved up to what was then high-tech, a Commmodore 128 computer with a color printer (for those of you who can follow this chronology by year, I'm dating myself quite a bit). After that I moved up to my first "real" personal computer and I have kept on file every liturgy, prayer, reflection, and random thought that I have ever put into electronic ink since then. I am grateful for the abundance of cheap storage media available today. The reason I keep all those files is because I use them. As I've mentioned before, there's no need to reinvent the wheel. I don't just recycle old liturgies; that would be an insult to God and the assembly. I often extract whatever elements were particularly useful and re-craft them into a new liturgy for a new occasion. When it comes to last-minute liturgies, I can take an existing liturgy for a related occasion and rework it quickly to suit a new need. In fact, believe it or not, while I was working on this section of the book, my phone rang. A colleague of mine, a director of music ministry who is a member of the LERT, called to declare a liturgical emergency. Seriously, we really do that! I was a bit surprised, as it was on a Sunday morning and it's unusual for us to be called out that early. I was due to meet her at church in a half hour and I couldn't imagine what couldn't wait until then. She said that Skippy-the-boy-priest (LERT-speak for newly ordained) was responsible for the Advent penance service the next day and when the pastor (who was scheduled to preach) asked for a copy of the service, Skippy looked puzzled and wondered aloud why anyone might need that. The pastor went ballistic and explained the error in his thinking. The emergency, it seemed, was well underway. There was no presider book, no readings selected, no music suggested, no examination of conscience considered, and no worship aid constructed. My friend asked if I might have a copy of any Advent penance service in my electronic files. Being the pack rat that I am, I have penance services dating back about fifteen years. I asked her what music she wanted to use and what the pastor wanted to preach about (so I could insert appropriate readings). I pulled up a relatively recent service from another parish, made the changes, polished the text a bit and in a little under an hour had a presider's book in a ceremonial binder of the appropriate color, an additional copy of the text for the presider's preparation, copies of the readings, a copy of the worship aid, and camera-ready originals of the worship aid for duplication. All that remained was to duplicate the worship aid and they were ready to go. Another successful LERT mission completed.

CHAPTER 4

Environment: Stuff to Use to Create a Prayerful Space and How to Arrange It

When preparing any liturgy, environment is an important component. It does not take extraordinary resources to provide an environment that appeals to many of the senses, even when planning time is very short. Because I work with liturgy a lot, I have a fair amount of liturgical "hardware" in my home that has served me well over the years. But even if you have only ordinary materials at your disposal, it's usually possible to add at least a bit of liturgical flavor to a prayer setting or service. I was once asked to help a religious community with a prayer service for a provincial meeting. I didn't have much notice for this, only a few hours. They were meeting in a high school building, so I knew that I would need something to help change the environment from a sense of business to a sense of prayer. It was springtime, early Easter season, so deciding what to do in terms of environment was fairly simple. I stopped by my local Pathmark on the way out and picked up a few small, inexpensive flowering plants and a white pillar candle. From home I brought with me a white tablecloth, a large-print book of the psalms, a clear bowl, a CD player, a couple of shoeboxes, a stapler, and what I like to think of as my "standard background music CD," Rufino Zaragoza's *A Sacred Place* (OCP, 1998).

Since this prayer would take place in the early evening, I would ordinarily have brought some incense with me, but knowing that the group would be praying in a school, I didn't want to take a chance on setting off smoke detectors. (That's an important point, by the way: Be careful about using candles, incense, or anything else that burns indoors. Smoke and heat detectors may be activated, but more importantly, you may create a safety hazard.) When I arrived I arranged an empty classroom into a prayer space. I arranged some chairs in a circle and lowered the shades halfway to filter the outside light. I set the CD player to repeat and turned the volume down very low to provide some subtle background. I put the shoeboxes on one of the classroom tables, creating two different levels, and draped the tablecloth over that, gathering it in swirls around the boxes and stapling the cloth unobtrusively to hold it in place. I placed the candle on top of the highest level, filled the bowl with water and set it on the second level, put the book in between, and arranged the plants. I opened the book to Psalm 118, lit the candle, and we were just about ready to go. It was still a classroom, but care had been taken to invite a sense of the sacred. These were just ordinary materials put to an extraordinary purpose.

If you find yourself preparing for liturgies, often you'll find yourself accumulating materials that make this easier.

PLANTS

Plants or other natural objects (stones, branches, sand, and so on) can contribute greatly to a prayerful environment. Even if you're preparing a prayer service at a meeting or other small gathering, including something of the outdoors can help to shift focus in a way that enables prayer. Sometimes it's helpful to bring something of the natural season indoors, as in the previous example. On the other hand, a contrast can be equally powerful, for example, using brightly colored flowers to form a contrast against the plain landscape of winter ordinary time. Some plants can convey a meaning that transcends season. If you include some sort of vine in a Christian prayer setting, it will generally evoke the image of John 15, the "vine and branches." Bare branches can convey a sense of barrenness; plants with thorns recall the passion. In short, the same principles that apply to the liturgical environment on a large and general scale apply to liturgies for which there is only a short time to prepare. The difference is that when you're working with limited resources and limited time, you need to be more creative with what you have on hand.

CANDLES

Candles are probably the simplest way to add a prayerful dimension to any situation. Candles carry a lot of symbolic weight. We light them in times of sadness and mourning, but we also light them in times of great joy. The flame is a source of warmth and comfort as well as being a good centering focus for prayer. Even the actual lighting of candles can have its own beauty. Among my collection of odd books is a very old pocket manual for altar boys (this was many years before the advent of female altar servers). It is a tiny book, with pages about 1 inches tall, designed to be hidden in the hands of altar boys who couldn't remember all of the Latin prayer responses. It includes a description of the various tasks during Mass, including lighting candles. It emphasizes that candlelight is a representation of Christ, the candles a reflection of divine purity, and that the very action of lighting the candles should be an event of beauty. There is definite beauty in a candlelight vigil, in the spreading of light from person to person. There is strength in the unity that light brings. Even a single candle can make that difference, reminding us of the light that shatters the darkness of our Easter vigiling. Bringing light into darkness satisfies a basic human need, offers hope, and helps to banish fear. If you are using a single candle, you can customize for the occasion if you have time. One of the ways that I have done this is to use an inkjet printer to print a graphic, text, or sometimes even a photographic image onto a large, clear adhesive label. You can generally apply this directly to the candle. Be careful, though, not to allow the candle to burn through the label. I prepared a memorial candle this way, applying an artist's rendering of the twin towers of the World Trade Center onto an ivory pillar candle. The colors of the towers were soft pastels. During November 2001, we displayed this candle surrounded by smaller votive candles bearing the names (I used smaller labels prepared the same way) of family, friends, and members of our community who had died in the attacks that September. It was a very simple yet elegant way to remember so many we had lost.

Lighting and Outdoor Issues

This covers a lot of environmental territory. Sometimes it requires just plain common sense. I know of a planning group who decided to put together a prayer service for the unborn at the last minute. Putting aside the fact that it's rarely a good idea to *choose* to do a liturgy at the last minute, particularly for such a sensitive issue, they didn't think their plan through. They wanted a candlelight service because they knew this had been effective for many other groups. They also wanted a good turnout, so they planned this service for ten o'clock on a Saturday morning. They meant well, but it makes no sense to have a candlelight service when the sun is doing a perfectly fine job of lighting the world. The unique nature of flickering candlelight in near-darkness was lost.

It's often possible to use lighting to your advantage. You may want to dim the lights or draw curtains or shades to focus on a particular image or flame (remember to leave enough light to read by, if need be). You may be able to use spotlights or other lights. You may want a brighter environment if your focus is on the dawn or the rising sun of hope, for example. Again, the principles of good liturgy should be your guide here. Don't make the mistake of thinking you need a dismal environment for a sad occasion.

If there's a good reason to pray outdoors, don't stay inside. One image that is burned in my memory is the sight of so many people from different faith backgrounds coming together outdoors on September 14, 2001, each holding a candle, many holding flags, all declaring that while we were a people injured, we were not broken. We could certainly have prayed indoors, we could even have prayed separately, but the power of the moment was outside. Sometimes you have to go where the prayer is.

The environment should fit the liturgy and the liturgy should fit the environmental context. Sometimes you won't have a choice of environment, but when you do, choose wisely. Remember that if you choose to pray outdoors, you may have to contend with weather conditions including wind and rain. I have had my music blow away during an outdoor evening prayer service; I now carry clothespins in my accompaniment books. A wise friend who had several versions of the *Order of Christian Funerals* destroyed as a result of many committal services in the rain gave me a very good suggestion. Photocopy the pages you need (of course, purchase the book first), put them upside-down in top-feeding plastic page protectors, and then tape the bottoms closed. That way, rain can't run onto the pages.

CENSERS

Incense has strong imagery. Some of our strongest memories are linked to smells and aromas. Burning incense appeals to both our sense of smell and our sense of sight. Although it is not always possible nor desirable to burn incense, it can add a unique dimension to prayer. Although a censer is something that may not be readily available, with a little effort, it can be constructed (at least for a one-time use) out of materials that are fairly common. If you have to construct one at the last minute, grab the watering tray from the bottom of an earthenware planter (one that is about six inches in diameter should work). Fill it with sand, granite chips, gravel, or even dirt if you have nothing else. If you can find a second tray that is about two inches in diameter, put that on top; if not, this will still work. Now you need charcoal and incense. The best type to use is the commercial self-lighting type found in church supply stores. You will only need about one half of one charcoal disk for this device; more than that may make it too warm to handle safely. Once the charcoal has burned to the point where ash has formed uniformly over the surface, you may drop one or two large grains of incense onto the charcoal. This will create sufficient incense for a small indoor gathering. I don't recommend using this outdoors, as any wind is likely to cause a problem.

If you intend to incense persons or objects with this, practice handling it in advance. There may be unanticipated hot spots. I saw this happen once at an archdiocesan evening prayer service in which a number of women religious were going to carry small metallic incense bowls out into the assembly. A few moments before they were to pick up the bowls, the table on which the bowls were prepared began to scorch. Wet towels had to be procured from the sacristy with great haste so that liturgy could continue in the usual way. Fortunately, in this case, the liturgist was heads-up enough to realize what had happened and react to it in time. Not so in a similar circumstance in which a liturgical dancer was processing with an incense brazier, tripped, and spilled hot coals all over the floor. She was barefoot, and the resulting procession took on the form of a fire dance. Sometimes, there just isn't a prayerful response to the unexpected.

If you have the opportunity (and the need) to use a thurible, either enlist the assistance of someone who is comfortable using it, or spend some time getting to know how it works. Handling red-hot objects on a chain is not quite as easy as it might seem. Here are some words of wisdom. With all incense-burning devices, clean the burn area before each use. Typically there is some residual incense left over and this will cause uneven burning and scorching with subsequent use. Don't use more charcoal than is necessary. This may cause overheating and make the device difficult to handle. If you intend to move about with it, practice walking until you find a comfortable rhythm. Don't swing the thurible aggressively nor lose control of the parts. People get hurt that way. If you can manage to handle incense well, you'll probably begin to look like you know exactly what you're doing.

UNDERSTANDING SYMBOLS

Part of knowing what you're doing means understanding symbols and using them well. Don't use empty symbols, don't use inappropriate symbols, and don't perpetuate the use of symbols that have lost their meaning. I worked in a parish where significant liturgical renewal was needed. I decided to focus my attention initially on the gathering rites and the entrance procession. The procession seemed to me to have an odd order and included elements that seemed out of place. When I inquired about the order (gently, of course!) I was told that the servers, readers, communion ministers, deacon, and priest lined up in that order because they were in order of importance. The servers were least important, followed by the reader, then the communion ministers, the deacon, and of course the priest, who was the most important of all. I never found out whose distorted theology taught them to think this way, but the symbolism spoke clearly to the assembly and as a result an entire community began to think of itself this way. Communion ministers saw themselves as superior to readers rather than as people with different gifts sharing liturgical ministry. One of the servers carried the sacramentary in procession. No one seemed to know exactly how this custom began, but one of the parish "elders" seemed to think it was so that the server who wasn't carrying the cross would have something to carry. There were then two books incorrectly carried in procession (they also processed with the lectionary, carried by the reader in the wrong place). When they reached the sanctuary, the server unceremoniously dumped the sacramentary onto the floor next to his chair. Although there was a great deal of symbolic action taking place here, almost none of it was positive.

One of the treasures of the Catholic tradition is the wealth of symbolism integrated into our liturgy. One of the best ways to develop fluency in the language of this symbolism is to study the eucharistic liturgy in terms of ritual. Susan Jorgensen's *Eucharist! An Eight-Session Ritual-Catechesis Experience for Adults* is a made-to-order method to learn the basics of ritual prayer. Using the eucharistic liturgy as a platform, Jorgensen explores ritual, symbol, song, and text from the gathering song through the dismissal. Along the way, symbols and language are experienced intimately. For example, while learning about the nature of symbols in the entrance rite, participants in this catechetical experience are invited to process into a worship space and to reverence the altar with a profound bow and a kiss. In my experience this is an enormously moving moment; most people have never imagined themselves engaging in that particular loving act. The result is that the next time they are gathered at an actual liturgy, their understanding of and participation in the presider's act of reverence take on a different dimension. This ritual-catechetical experience is a phenomenal teaching tool and is a great place to start to learn about the dynamics of the ritual experience. It helps a lot to have some of that information tucked away in your mind so that, when the unexpected happens, you have a chance of responding in a way that looks like you know what you're doing.

Chapter 5

How to Look Like You Know Exactly What You're Doing

Sometimes a response to the unexpected occurs not in the form of a liturgy but *during* a liturgy. Usually, the best way to respond is to look like you know what you're doing. This is true regardless of the role you happen to take in any given liturgy. Here's an example. I was a liturgy coordinator in a parish celebrating confirmation one year during the Easter season. Like any good coordinator, I'd gone over my checklist twice, made sure that all the unusual items unique to a liturgy with a bishop presider were in place, checked the ritual books, the vessels, the lemons (for removing oil from the hands), and so on. Somehow, at just about the time the procession reached the sanctuary, I realized that I'd neglected to light the paschal candle. This particular bishop had a reputation for being a stickler for details, I had a reputation of being a perfectionist, and my parish had a reputation of having high standards for liturgy. The bishop's master of ceremonies was giving me the liturgical death glare from across the room, and I was imagining how I'd feel later that day, impaled on my own paschal candle, when I had an idea. I would make this appear deliberate. Just as the bishop concluded his homily and prepared to begin the renewal of baptismal promises, I picked up a large taper, and purposefully lit it. The music minister saw what I was about to do (she, too, had seen the liturgical death glare) and played a fanfare on the organ. I stepped up to the candle, lit it gently, the music tapered down to a whisper, and the renewal of baptismal promises followed in the light of the paschal candle. Then, as we say, Mass continued in the usual way. This story illustrates a number of important points.

KNOW WHAT COMES NEXT.

I had made a mistake for certain. Failing to light the paschal candle for a rite of initiation on a Sunday during the Easter season is pretty hard to miss. But because I knew what came next, I knew where in the rite a correction of the error would fit best. I was lucky because there happened to be a ritual break that allowed for this; that's not always the case. But by knowing the ritual well, I was able to escape what might have been an awkward situation.

ACT AND MOVE WITH PURPOSE.

When I teach people how to preside or serve at liturgy, I stress deliberate motion. Good liturgy demands that we speak, move, and act with care. When things start to go wrong, if you move with dignity and grace, you can do almost anything at liturgy and have it appear as though it were planned rather than a response to the unexpected. If I had tried to sneak over to the paschal candle and light it without being noticed, all I would have accomplished would have been to call attention to myself and to the fact that the candle was unlit. By moving purposefully, I made it seem as though the lighting of the candle at that moment was nothing out of the ordinary. Also, because I was supervising the young people serving the liturgy, I was vested, as were all the other ministers in the sanctuary. This sometimes makes me nearly invisible (I work hard at blending into the background!) but has the added effect of causing people to believe that if I'm up there, and I'm not moving frantically about, I must know what I'm doing. The end result was that we turned an error in preparation into a focus on an initiation rite. It wouldn't have been my choice to do it that way, and I wasn't trying to trick anyone. I'm not suggesting that we deliberately try to deceive people, but sometimes maintaining the flow of liturgy requires a little misdirection. Which leads to the next point: liturgical awareness.

BE AWARE OF WHAT'S GOING ON AROUND YOU.

If you have to make an unplanned move, try to do it when something else is moving. You're less likely to be noticed if, for example, the assembly is changing posture at the same time that you're moving about. In this case, I moved at the same time that the bishop and all of his ministers were moving (he would need book, mitre, and bucket for the next bit of ritual). The music covered whatever confusion this might have caused otherwise and it was all over very quickly. Another very important factor here is being aware of other people in leadership roles. The music minister (who happens to be a LERT member) and I are accustomed to working together, so a glance or a gesture can speak volumes. She knew as soon as I started to move that something wasn't quite right, and I only had to glance up at the candle for her to get the picture. We used to joke that one priest that we worked with could direct an entire liturgy using only his eyes. Some said he could move his eyeballs independently of each other to more efficiently orchestrate the liturgical flow. In any case, keep the connection with others involved in the liturgy intact. It's important, even if the unexpected never happens.

What if an actual, real-life emergency happens just as liturgy is about to begin? Do you stop the liturgy? Send people away? Continue as if nothing happened? Perhaps all of the above? There's no single answer to that question. Each situation demands its own answer. Here's one example: Moments before the beginning of a late summer Mass was to begin, an older woman of my community suffered a heart attack in the gathering area. An emergency medical services unit was summoned by one of the ushers. As all of this was happening, people in the worship space became restless; Mass had always started on time and no one knew what was the cause of the delay. Hearing sirens, I followed one of the nuns in our parish (who happens to be a nurse) out to the vestibule to see what was wrong. Sister went over to the crowd around the victim, shook her head, came back and croaked loudly into my ear, "She's dead!" and began to pray. Stunned, I went back inside and told the music minister what had happened. We agreed that the best thing we could do was to explain the situation in general terms to the assembly and invite them to pray together. So, taking a deep breath, I stepped up to the microphone and explained that a woman in our parish had suffered a heart attack just outside, that paramedics were working to resuscitate her, and that the pastor (who was to have been the presider that evening) and other ministers were praying for her now. I did not mention what sister had said. I invited them to pray silently for her and then to join in song. Together we sang the psalm that we were to sing for that Mass. When we finished, I again heard the sirens and seeing that the ministers were lined up and ready to go, we began Mass in the usual way. When we got to the responsorial psalm, the assembly sang it with amazing passion and power, recalling, I believe, the reason we sang it earlier that evening. During the homily, the pastor explained what had happened and said that the paramedics had been able to revive the woman and that she was conscious and responsive by the time they were ready to transport her to the hospital. I was more than a little astounded at that revelation and very glad that I had said nothing at all regarding the woman's condition when I gave my explanation. Again, I learned from the experience.

PEOPLE WILL PRAY WHEN THERE'S SOMETHING TO PRAY ABOUT AND A WAY TO DO IT.

This was a situation that was a complete no-brainer. We were already gathered for prayer, an event occurred that was evocative of prayer, the environment and the method were in place, and the people wanted to do it. I remember that instant so clearly. The question was never *should* we pray; the only question was how best could we quickly and sensitively enter into this particular prayerful response to the unexpected. If we had only asked them to remain seated and to pray silently, the whole room would have been in chaos within about a minute. That request only works well with a group well disciplined with silence — a group of contemplatives, for example. Everyone else begins to fidget. Praying in song is something familiar, and singing a familiar psalm opens the door gently to common prayer. The psalms contain texts for every moment of life: joy, sadness, fear, change, uncertainty, wonder, remorse … the list goes on. They make up a big piece of the liturgical tool kit. Learn the psalms. The easiest way to do this is to learn to sing them; they were meant to be sung. If you commit psalms to memory, you'll never be at a loss for a prayer text when you need one. And on a personal note, if you learn the psalms you'll never be at a loss for prayer even in times of tragedy when you think you have no more words.

Someone has to lead.

Someone has to make the decision about what the response to the unexpected event is going to be. In retrospect, it amuses me that I even had to think for a millisecond about what to do in this situation. I remember looking at my friend at the keyboard and knowing that we had a responsibility to lead that assembly in prayer as we are called to do. Learn how to lead. Your baptism demands it.

Never listen to anything that anyone croaks in your ear.

This is good advice both in liturgy and life. Actually, a more important axiom would be, "Be careful how you pray." Someone far wiser than I once watched me struggle to craft intercessions for an anniversary celebration for a friend. I was trying very hard to make sure each word was perfect. He told me that the most important part of the art of creating prayer was to communicate an image worthy of the assembly's "Amen." In other words, pray the truth. In this case, thankfully, I didn't go beyond what I knew to be true. I didn't say that the woman was dead because I didn't know that to be true. I did not invite prayers for her soul nor for her recovery. Prayer isn't about telling God what to do; it's about acknowledging that we need God.

I'm a good example of what needing God is all about. I must have a sign on my head that flashes "pick me" in neon lights, because despite my best attempts at blending into the woodwork, folks always seem to ask me to pray for someone, bless something, or lead prayer for some occasion. One such occasion happened many years ago at a reception following a Greek Orthodox baptism. It was my first experience of an Eastern Rite baptism and I was intrigued by how large and full their

symbols were and how greatly involved the community was in the
initiation of this child. After the baptism, family, friends, and (it
seemed) half the parish gathered at a nearby reception hall for a grand
party. The guest of honor and his parents were delayed a bit by the
photographer, and while we were waiting, a number of us had gathered
at the bar. A few drinks later, the child's mother rushed in and asked if
she could speak with me for a moment. As I stood up, my head started
to spin a bit as I followed her a bit unsteadily out of the room. She told
me that their priest had been called away on an emergency and asked if
I would say grace before dinner. I enthusiastically agreed, feeling
honored and touched that they would ask me. I was also fairly young at
the time, relatively new to ministry, and more than a little bit buzzed.
This qualified as an unexpected event. Being young and not as sober as
I should have been (in retrospect), I didn't consider the effect that the
substitution of a short, black Roman Catholic woman for a Greek
Orthodox priest might have on the friends and family gathered there. I
was certain that I could get through something as simple as saying grace
without ruffling too many feathers. Apparently I was mistaken. What
followed was an example of God's unfailing mercy. The mother of the
newly baptized introduced me, and as I walked up to the microphone I
glanced over at the child's grandmother. She seemed to be inflating
before my very eyes. It was very, very clear to me that she was not
happy about this development. I started out with a very simple, "Let us
pray…," and with that, Grandma looked about ready to explode. I did
the only thing I could think of at the time. I thanked God for his
presence and asked his blessing on the most handsome and wonderful
child that was such a source of joy to his parents and grandparents
(Grandma deflated a bit at that). I thought that almost no mother
could resist that. I prayed that he would make his parents proud of

him, in the same way that they had honored their parents before them. After that, I lost track. I know I included the godparents and the aunts and uncles (all children of the maternal grandparents) in the blessings and that there was immediate dancing as soon as we stopped praying. Everyone was happy and people were hugging me and thanking me for my beautiful words. I had no idea what I said, but it must have been the right thing. Fifteen years later, people still tell me how wonderful that one prayer was and I remember almost nothing of it other than that it was a joyous celebration of life. I was scared, but somehow I managed to speak words that reached people. I learned several valuable lessons that day.

DON'T DRINK AND PRAY.

This particular truth was imparted to me by a pastor under whom I worked for a time. We were out at a restaurant for a staff dinner meeting one night and he had ordered a beer, but then quickly changed the order to a soda. When we teased him about it, he said he had to lead prayer at another meeting later that evening, and he had learned from experience not to drink at all before doing so. When I thought back on my own experience, I had to agree. It's hard enough to control what comes out of your mouth when sober; putting alcohol into the mix doesn't help any.

KNOW WHAT YOU'RE GETTING INTO.

The baptism was a situation in which I was something of a poor fit for what was needed. With more experience in ministry under my belt, I would have chosen a different option. I probably would have offered to write a simple form of grace that the father of the newly baptized could read. I definitely would not have risked offending any part of that wonderful family by my presence or action. And with a glass or two of wine in me I should have had the good sense to try to find another way to accommodate their needs. Responding to the unexpected doesn't mean plunging headfirst into the crisis of the hour.

Don't assume a role you can't fill.

Grandma was expecting a priest. It makes no difference to her that a layperson in my tradition or theirs is perfectly capable of saying grace before a meal. That really was all I intended to do. This brings up the very important topic of who can do what at prayer.

Who can do what at prayer?

In a general sense, anyone may lead prayer and anyone may share the good news. That is not the same as saying that anyone may preside and anyone may proclaim and preach the Gospel. It's important to know the difference. Here's an example. A non-Catholic friend called me and asked if I could do a funeral service for her friend's mother. My first question was what sort of service did they need and what faith tradition was the family of the deceased. As it turned out, the deceased and the family were Catholic, but the mother had been living in an assisted-living facility quite far from the family and had no faith community there. The family was not active. It seems they were at a loss as to what to do about the funeral, so they had a friend call me. For me, this situation was simple. I spoke with a family member and offered to work with a local funeral home and a parish close to them to make appropriate arrangements, and I offered the support of my team in preparing the vigil and funeral liturgies. I explained that, while I could not preside, I could work closely with a priest who would be able to do that for them and that other team members were available for music ministry and ministry of the word. If they wished, I would lead prayer at the wake and at the graveside, but I pointed out that if the family was not particularly active, it might be disruptive to have a layperson in that role. This type of situation requires some sensitivity. At one time, I might have jumped at the chance to preside, thinking that since it was permissible I should take the opportunity. With a lot more experience, however, I know now that the easiest thing to do (in this case, presiding myself) is not always the most pastoral thing to do.

VARIOUS FORMS OF BLESSING — ORDAINED VS. LAY (OR HOW NOT TO OFFEND THE LITURGICAL POLICE)

I remember the very first time I presided at Morning Prayer. It was long before I had begun to include the Liturgy of the Hours as part of my personal prayer on any kind of regular basis, and I really did not know the structure of this prayer form very well (strike one). I had been asked to preside for Holy Thursday morning, but the ritual had not been given to me in advance because, in the words of the liturgy coordinator at the time, "It's too simple to worry about preparing in advance" (strike two). Because I didn't have very much time to prepare, I didn't look carefully at the beginning and ending of each segment of the prayer as laid out in the presider's book (strike three). I was already out before I stepped up to the plate. Actually, the prayer went very well, much better than I had anticipated, until we got to the very end. I prayed the collect at the end of the Lord's Prayer, turned the page and realized that there was nothing else in the book. I hadn't a clue how to end this thing! I didn't know the formulary for this prayer and even if I had, the worship aid for the assembly did not include a response for this unusual ritual dialogue. Not knowing what to do, and running out of time, I went into Catholic reflex mode. I knew that if I used the formulary for concluding Mass, they would respond appropriately and I could get out of there with some semblance of dignity. So I said. "The Lord be with you ..." and finished with "Go in peace." I got out of there with a relatively prayerful response to something that was entirely unexpected on my part, but the liturgical police just about crucified me for it. What I had done, and I was too inexperienced at the time to realize it, was use a ritual dialogue construction restricted to use by the ordained; this is, as I learned, a capital offense. There was genuine outrage by the clergy, one of whom was responsible for constructing the presider's book without the appropriate closing. How dare I use such a construction! What was I thinking? How could I possibly not know how to end Morning Prayer? On and on it went. That was just the beginning of a continuing problem with ritual constructions. A layperson at liturgy may not express the desire that the Lord might be with the assembly, nor may a layperson dismiss the assembly with the instruction to go in peace. This becomes problematic when using a prayer form that is unfamiliar to the assembly. I know that I could stand up on an airplane and say "The Lord be with you" in a commanding voice, and every Catholic asleep on that plane would wake up, say "And also with you," and go back to sleep. Our corporate identity allows us to speak this way. If instead I said, as the ordinary for Morning Prayer instructs, "May the Lord bless us, protect us from all evil and bring us to everlasting life," all I would get would be blank looks and perhaps a set of handcuffs.

A similar problem arises in the orders for blessing of the sick. A priest or deacon may use familiar ritual dialogue to begin the blessing. He signs and greets in the usual way. In response to the signing, the people respond as they ordinarily do, with "Amen," and to the greeting of peace, with "And also with you." In contrast, a lay minister uses the construction, "Brothers and sisters, let us bless the Lord, who went about doing good and healing the sick. Blessed be God now and for ever," to which the community is somehow supposed to know to respond, "Blessed be God now and for ever" or "Amen" (BB 382).

There is no legal solution to these awkward elements, but it is important to know that they are there so that you can be prepared to deal with them. One way of dealing with problematic dialogue is to plant someone who knows the correct response into the assembly so that someone can respond to greetings and the like that seem to have no obvious response. There is, of course, a genuine concern about misrepresentation. The argument is that, by using dialogue customarily used by the ordained, members of the faithful, laypeople may inadvertently (or perhaps in some cases, intentionally) mislead the assembly into perceiving them as clergy. Whether or not this is a reasonable argument is not the issue here. The important principle to follow is to do no harm. God's people are never well served by power struggles, particularly regarding prayer. Be careful about the words you choose. Don't presume that, because you've heard a phrase used, it may be used by anyone.

It's not always easy to know what words to use, what can be blessed by whom, and who can preside over what. One way to become familiar with the general forms is to read through some of the introductions in the *Book of Blessings*. It does a good job of describing the different text and postures to be used by lay versus ordained presiders as well as indicating where only an ordained presider is appropriate. It is sometimes difficult, though, to extrapolate from this. Laypeople can bless some objects but not others. They can bless Advent wreaths but not rosaries (although a rosary is blessed by its use). They can bless people at some times but not at other times. They can bless children, but not married couples. A fairly safe rule of thumb for laypersons is to avoid blessing religious articles, avoid blessing food other than your own meal, and when it comes to blessing people, look it up. The rules on that vary too much to make a general statement about them. A last-minute liturgy requires some flexibility, despite all the rules in all the books. Pastoral sensitivity is important here.

Other Things That Help

Sticky Notes and Binders

Pastoral sensitivity is important, but sticky notes are essential. Sticky notes and ceremonial binders have a place of honor in my liturgical arsenal. Ceremonial binders are great because I can rework an existing ritual or create a new one, put it in a binder, and never have to worry about page turns or ribbons that slip out. I can make certain that everyone involved in a liturgy is on the same page if all they have is the same page. It's a lot harder to make a mistake in coordination when everyone is working from the same script. This is particularly true in last-minute situations when a ritual may be unfamiliar and there is no time for a run-through. It's also very easy to provide binders for different ministers that are prepared for their specific needs. At the very least, when I put together binders for liturgy, I put in page breaks where a natural break in the ritual occurs. It won't be in the same place for the presider as for the reader, for example. If I need to include the readings (I use the proper ritual book whenever possible) they appear in large type for the reader and the line breaks correspond to phrasing. Being attentive to these details makes any ritual flow more naturally. Beyond that, binders that are coordinated with liturgical environment or color add a touch of dignity. It says that preparation was done with care. Although binders intended for liturgical use can be expensive, they're worth the investment if you work with liturgy on a regular basis. In general, any type of binder is preferable to a handful of papers stapled together. I always cringe when I see a reader approach the ambo only to take a crumpled piece of paper out of a jacket pocket from which to read. It's hard to find a sense of proclamation in that.

The sticky notes simply spare me from making mistakes. I use small sticky notes anywhere I need to use a name that might be forgotten. I always include the names on these notes in the baptism, wedding, and funeral ritual books, no matter how well the presider knows the names. Anyone can have a momentary brain stall and forget a name. Just having it there, needed or not, will generally make a presider more comfortable. I also like to use the clear type with colored arrows on them to indicate the selected form of a prayer or a reading. It makes it hard to lose your place. I had an experience once in which a priest presiding at a baptism became confused and prayed both forms of the renunciation of sin in sequence. Apparently, he hadn't noticed that this prayer came in the [A, B] format, so we all renounced sin and rejected Satan twice. Apparently detecting some residual sin, we all did it one more time along with the parents and godparents. After all, Satan can never be rejected too many times.

Networking and Using Resources

There's a recurring theme here, and that is to avoid trying to do everything yourself. Sometimes you don't have a choice, but when there's an opportunity to get help from people whose talents differ from or complement your own, take it. We all bring different gifts to prayer; God wants us to use them. If you're faced with a last-minute situation don't assume that it's too late to ask for help. Chances are, someone will have what you need. If you're trying to prepare a service of some sort and you're not a pastoral musician, call one. If you explain the nature of the liturgical emergency, a competent pastoral musician can help you, especially if you ask the right questions. For example, if you're preparing an evening prayer of thanksgiving for a community who survived a crisis and you need a psalm that speaks of gratitude, that pastoral musician will probably come up with a setting of one of the psalms of praise, perhaps Psalm 30 or 67. You can work backward from there to construct your service. Look up those two psalms in the Liturgy of the Hours and see which psalm prayer corresponds to it. See if the reading and intercessions fit. Chances are that they will. If not, ask someone who preaches well about an appropriate reading; such people tend to know Scripture very well. See if the evening hymn fits as well. If not, go to your music resource of choice (or ask the same pastoral musician you asked about the psalm), look in the index under "praise," "thanksgiving," or "gratitude," and pick one. After that, you're pretty well set. If you need a worship aid, ask someone who does page layout regularly to help out; better still, ask someone who does worship aids regularly. That person may already have the components you need.

Easy Worship Aids

Worship aids have gone through a long, often torturous process of evolution. Thankfully, they are no longer typewritten, photocopied sheets of paper handed out to an unsuspecting assembly. They have a genuine function at liturgy and may be particularly helpful in a last-minute environment. As with all else at liturgy, a worship aid must be designed with care and sensitivity and must in every way be worthy of the liturgy and of the assembly it serves. A well-designed worship aid will support and encourage the direct participation of those who gather in prayer while at the same time reflect the needs and character of the assembled community. It's the simplest way of providing the necessary texts, music, and other resources in a clear format, in a single location, allowing the assembly to focus its attention on the liturgy. If all you really need is a program, don't bother putting together a worship aid. They serve distinct and separate purposes. Programs help spectators to follow a performance, and liturgy is never a performance.

The primary purpose of a worship aid is to assist the assembly in taking a full and active role in liturgy. Issues such as gender inclusivity and sensitivity to local custom must be carefully considered to avoid offending any of those who come together in prayer. Simplicity of design, as well as careful attention to typography and artwork, will ensure that attention remains focused where it belongs — on the worship rather than the aid. Any office supply store can provide good quality paper at a low cost. Inexpensive computer equipment can produce photographic-quality printing. Photocopying (last-minute liturgies rarely leave time for other methods) is inexpensive as well and produces a serviceable result. None of these should be an impediment to preparing a worship aid. When preparing a liturgy or service that may be somewhat unfamiliar to some of the participants, the worship aid might include some brief explanation of the ritual or text as well as indications for posture. People feel much more comfortable if they know when to sit, stand, or kneel. Including any necessary music is helpful as well. Probably the single most important guideline is that of simplicity. Don't include any unnecessary text; doing this encourages people to read along rather than listen and participate in a more active way. The rites and rituals of the church are filled with a wealth of powerful imagery, and the signs and symbols should speak clearly of themselves. Explaining them away only dilutes this power. In the same way, if you're constructing a unique service, whatever symbols you use should speak clearly.

Use type that is clear, easy to read, and that will reproduce well. Remember to consider lighting when you prepare. If you're preparing a candlelight service, don't use gray text on off-white paper; nobody can see that by the light of a candle. With all of the styles of type available, it is tempting to go overboard, but fancy type can be distracting. Don't use decorative typestyles that are difficult to read. For body text, choose a style that is simple and elegant and clearly legible after duplication. Choose a size that can be read clearly. Select no more than two styles that work well together and stick with them.

A word about copyrights. Don't use copyrighted material without permission. This is a very simple concept that seems to elude many people. If, for example, you prepare a worship aid with copyrighted material, all you need to do in most cases is call or e-mail the publisher and ask for permission. They may charge a fee. Generally they will give you permission over the phone or by return e-mail. In some cases there will not be a charge for a single use, but this cannot be assumed to be so. Paying attention to copyright issues is a matter of justice.

There are already too few liturgical composers and artists, and they deserve to be compensated for their work. By reproducing their work without acknowledging them nor paying for the rights, we deny them a just wage.

How to Get People Involved

This is simple. Ask them. Especially in a situation in which there is a sudden and shared emotion, people are often grateful for the chance to "do" something. After the immediate shock of the first hours of September 11, 2001, people searched desperately for some way to help. They gathered at what came to be called "ground zero" to help the rescue attempt that all too soon became a recovery attempt. They lined up at blood banks and firehouses and, not surprisingly, at churches. I know many stories like this, but one stands out in my mind. When the leadership of one particular church indicated that the workers at ground zero were becoming dehydrated and needed water and other fluids, people went to stores and bought out the total supply of drinks on the shelves. Then they did something quite unusual. They prayed together and they blessed all those cases of drinks before they packed them up and sent them into the city. There was a presider, a reader, and a song leader. None of these had ever served in ministry. When asked to lead in a time of crisis, they didn't hesitate in action, nor did they hesitate in prayer. Leaders are there. Sometimes it takes a certain moment in time for their gifts to be revealed.

Conclusion

Prayerful Responses to the Unexpected

Although there are many possible liturgical responses to the unexpected, the overall thought process in achieving the response is similar. If the unexpected happens *during* liturgy, your best chance at responding prayerfully is in being well prepared for the liturgy before it begins. When preparing a liturgy in response to the unexpected, the following process is a guide to achieving a prayerful response:

- **Determine what is happening or what has happened.** Is this an emergency situation or something less urgent? Is the need immediate or will you have time to prepare? Does the situation impact an individual, group, community, or a larger group? If it is a group, what is the faith composition?

- **Decide if a response is needed.** Why are you praying and what are you praying about? Who will be praying? What do you need from God in this time and place? Having answered that, what form of prayer will you use to best serve God's people at this moment?

- **Consider the desired outcome.** If there is an existing format for the desired outcome, use or adapt it. How will you draw people into prayer, toward God, and toward each other? What will people need to make this prayer their own? What will speak to all their senses? What will help them to express their sadness, joy, confusion, pain, triumph? What will be changed when you have concluded your prayer? How will you sing prayer? Do you need any other ritual or symbol with which to begin? Do you need a particular gathering rite or introduction of some sort? What form will the rest of the ritual take?

- **Gather your team and assemble resources using sound liturgical principles.** Having decided on a prayer form, what ministers do you need? Who will preside, proclaim, and lead song? What words will you use, what imagery will you form? What sort of environment will best support this prayer?

- **Finally, respond in an authentic way to the unexpected event.** Remember in all your preparation to trust that "where two or three are gathered in my name, there am I in the midst of them" (Mt 18:20).

God is always present. Even at the last minute, and always in the unexpected.

Catella, Alceste. "Theology of Liturgy." In *Handbook for Liturgical Studies: Fundamental Liturgy*, edited by A. Chupungco, 3–28. Collegeville, Minn.: The Liturgical Press, 1998.

Cervera, Jésus C. "Liturgy and Symbolism." In *Handbook for Liturgical Studies: Fundamental Liturgy*, edited by A. Chupungco, 45–64. Collegeville, Minn.: The Liturgical Press, 1998.

Collins, Mary. *Contemplative Participation*. Collegeville, Minn.: The Liturgical Press, 1990.

Corbon, Jean. *The Wellspring of Worship*. New York: Paulist Press, 1988.

Crichton, J.D. "A Theology of Worship." In *The Study of Liturgy*, edited by C. Jones, et al. 3–31. New York: Oxford University Press, 1992.

Guardini, Romano. *The Church and the Catholic*. New York: Sheed & Ward, 1953.

Hovda, Robert. "Vesting of Liturgical Ministers." *Worship* 54.4 (1980): 363–368.

Kavanagh, Aidan. *On Liturgical Theology*. Collegeville, Minn.: The Liturgical Press, 1984.

Lathrop, Gordon W. *Holy Things: A Liturgical Theology*. Minneapolis: Fortress Press, 1993.

Saliers, Don E. *Worship and Spirituality*. Philadelphia: Westminster, 1984.

Book of Blessings. Collegeville, Minn: The Liturgical Press, 1989.

The Book of Common Prayer. Kingston, Tenn.: Kingsport Press, 1977.

Catholic Household Blessings & Prayers. Washington, D.C.: United States Conference of Catholic Bishops, 1989.

Ford-Grabowsky, Mary. *Prayers for All People.* New York: Doubleday, 1995.

Holy Communion and the Worship of Eucharist Outside Mass. Totowa, N.J.: Catholic Book Publishing Company, 1991.

Hughes, Kathleen. *Lay Presiding: The Art of Leading Prayer.* Collegeville, Minn: The Liturgical Press, 1991.

Jorgensen, Susan. *Eucharist: An Eight-Session Ritual-Catechesis Experience for Adults.* San Jose, Calif.: Resource Publications, Inc., 1994.

Liturgy of the Hours. New York: Catholic Book Publishing Company, 1976.

Order of Christian Funerals. Totowa, N.J.: Catholic Book Publishing Company, 1998.

Pastoral Care of the Sick. New York: Catholic Book Publishing Company, 1983.

Prayers for Sundays and Seasons. Chicago: Liturgy Training Publications, 1998.

Remembering the Women: Women's Stories from Scripture for Sundays and Festivals. Chicago: Liturgy Training Publications, 1999.

A Ritual for Laypersons: Rites for Holy Communion and the Pastoral Care of the Sick and Dying. Collegeville, Minn.: The Liturgical Press, 1993.

More Resources from Donna Cole

LITURGICAL MINISTRY
A Practical Guide to Spirituality
Donna Cole
Paper, $8.95
64 pages, 5½" x 8½"
0-89390-372-8

Support and affirm your volunteer liturgical ministers with this concise and practical book on spirituality. *Liturgical Ministry* is full of practical tips specific to lectors, ministers of communion, musicians, ministers of hospitality, and servers.

MINISTRY & LITURGY MAGAZINE
Donna Cole, editor
10 issues per year

Group subscriptions available

Ministry & Liturgy is a professional magazine for the whole parish ministry team. Each issue is dedicated to the vital work of pastoral ministry and to meeting the challenge of preparing vibrant liturgy. To receive a risk-free subscription, contact Resource Publications, Inc., and receive your first issue followed by an invoice. If you like what you see, return the invoice with your payment; if you choose not to subscribe, just mark "No thanks" on the invoice and return it. The first issue is yours to keep.

Order these resources from your local bookseller
or call 1-888-273-7782 (toll-free) or 1-408-286-8505
or visit the Resource Publications, Inc., website at www.rpinet.com.